Why Money Matters

Family income, poverty and children's lives

Edited by Jason Strelitz and Ruth Lister

"*Save the Children's new book,* Why Money Matters, *is a powerful reminder of the impact low incomes have on the lives of children living in poverty. Between 1998/99 and 2005/06, 600,000 children have been lifted out of relative poverty and 1.8 million children have been lifted out of absolute poverty, and increasing employment opportunities and reform of financial support for families have made a major contribution to this. We are committed to tackling child poverty and I welcome the contribution this book makes.*"

Rt Hon Alistair Darling MP, Chancellor of the Exchequer

We're the world's independent children's charity.
We're outraged that millions of children are still denied
proper healthcare, food, education and protection.
We're working flat out to get every child their rights
and we're determined to make further, faster changes.
How many? How fast? It's up to you.

Published by
Save the Children
1 St John's Lane
London EC1M 4AR
UK
+44 (0)20 7012 6400
savethechildren.org.uk

First published 2008

Registered Company No. 178159

Authors have contributed individual chapters and do not necessarily agree with everything that is said in other chapters.

Typeset by Grasshopper Design Company
Printed by Page Bros (Norwich) Ltd

Save the Children publications are printed on paper sourced from sustainable forests.

Contents

Part 2
Poverty: the impact on well-being

Part 3
Ensuring a decent income for all

Conclusion
Towards eradicating child poverty

Note on contributors

Brendan Barber is General Secretary of the Trades Union Congress (TUC), which represents 59 unions with a total membership of around 6.5 million people working in all sectors of the economy. He joined the TUC in 1975, becoming Head of the Press Department in 1979 and Head of the Industrial Relations Department in 1987, before being appointed Deputy General Secretary in 1993. He was elected General Secretary in 2003 and has served on a number of public bodies, including the ACAS (Advisory, Conciliation and Arbitration Service) Council. He is currently a Non-Executive Director of the Court of the Bank of England.

Fran Bennett is a Senior Research Fellow at the Department of Social Policy and Social Work, University of Oxford, where she teaches and carries out research, especially policy analysis. She has a particular interest in poverty, social security and gender issues. She also works in a self-employed capacity on similar issues, often for non-governmental organisations or think-tanks. She has in the past been director of the Child Poverty Action Group (CPAG), and has been a policy adviser to Oxfam on UK and European poverty issues.

Jonathan Bradshaw CBE is Professor of Social Policy at the University of York. His current research includes national and international comparative studies of child well-being; minimum income standards; and the social exclusion of young people. He is a UK expert on the European Union National Action Plans for Social Inclusion, an adviser to the Work and Pensions Committee and Chair of York Welfare Benefits Unit.

Tania Burchardt is a Senior Research Fellow at the Centre for Analysis of Social Exclusion at the London School of Economics. Her research interests include the economic and social exclusion of disabled people, welfare policy, and theories of social justice. She is editor of *Benefits: The journal of poverty and social justice*, and is currently working on a volume entitled *Social Justice and Public Policy: Seeking fairness in diverse societies*, co-edited with David Gordon and Gary Craig.

Matt Davies is National Coordinator of ATD Fourth World, a voluntary organisation working alongside people living in long-term poverty to support them in their refusal to accept poverty as a fact of life and find the solutions to eradicate it together. Prior to being posted to London, Matt worked for ATD Fourth World in Guatemala, Madrid and at their International Centre in Paris.

Elizabeth Dowler is a Registered Public Health Nutritionist and Reader in Food and Social Policy in the Department of Sociology at the University of Warwick, where she works on food, nutrition, poverty and policy. She and Nick Spencer edited *Challenging Health Inequalities: From Acheson to 'Choosing Health'* in 2007 for Policy Press.

Paul Gregg is a Professor in the Department of Economics, University of Bristol. He is also a member of the London Child Poverty Commission and a Programme Director at the Centre for Market and Public Organisation. He was formally a member of the Council of Economic Advisers at HM Treasury 1997–2006, where he worked on welfare reform and child poverty.

Lesley Hoggart is a Senior Research Fellow at the Policy Studies Institute. She specialises in qualitative research and is currently the project leader of the qualitative research strand of the Employment Retention and Advancement (ERA) evaluation. Her research interests include lone parents, young mothers, teenage pregnancy, and social inclusion and education.

Claire Kober is Head of Policy and Campaigns at the Family Welfare Association. Prior to this she worked for a major disability charity where she managed the policy team. She has a particular interest in poverty and social exclusion issues and formerly worked for the Campaign to End Child Poverty. Claire is a local councillor in North London.

Stephen Lea is a Professor of Psychology at the University of Exeter, where he has worked since 1976. He has been carrying out research into economic psychology for more than 30 years, and is a past President of the International Association for Research in Economic Psychology. From an initial focus on decision-making, he developed a long-standing interest in the psychological causes and impacts of debt, poverty and homelessness. He also works on areas like the psychology of money and gift-giving, as well as pursuing a quite separate set of interests in animal behaviour.

Ruth Lister CBE, AcSS, is Professor of Social Policy at Loughborough University. She is a former Director of the Child Poverty Action Group and author of *Poverty* (Polity Press, 2004).

Stephen McKay is Professor of Social Research at the University of Birmingham, and until 2007 was Deputy Director of the Personal Finance Research Centre at Bristol. He principally conducts quantitative research investigating how incomes vary across different groups, and the importance of wealth, savings and debts. In 2007 he co-authored a report for the Fawcett Society that compared the savings and debts of men and women.

Avril Mewse is a Senior Lecturer at the University of Exeter. Her research interests span health, social, and economic psychology. She has a long-standing interest in the health behaviours of young people, and has been involved in research examining the impact of debt, poverty and homelessness. She also has research interests in recidivist offending behaviour and domestic violence.

David Piachaud is Professor of Social Policy at the London School of Economics and an Associate of the Centre for Analysis of Social Exclusion (CASE). He was Social Policy Adviser in the Prime Minister's Policy Unit (1974–79) and has been Consultant to the European Commission, the International Labour Organization and the OECD (Organisation for Economic Co-operation and Development). He has written papers and books on children, poverty, social security, social exclusion and social policy.

Gabrielle Preston is Policy and Research Officer at CPAG. Her publications include *Helter Skelter: Families, disabled children and the benefit system* (CASE paper 92, 2006) and *Out of Reach: Benefits for disabled children* (with Mark Robinson) (CPAG, 2006). She has also edited *At Greatest Risk: The children most likely to be poor* (CPAG, 2005) and *A Route Out of Poverty: Disabled people, work and welfare reform* (CPAG, 2006).

Karen Rowlingson is Professor of Social Policy and Director of Research at the Institute of Applied Social Studies at the University of Birmingham. Research interests include inequality and poverty; wealth and riches; personal finances and asset-based welfare.

Jason Strelitz is Save the Children's Policy Adviser on UK Child Poverty, working as part of the Campaign to End Child Poverty to eradicate child poverty in the UK. He has previously completed his PhD at the Centre for the Analysis of Social Exclusion at the London School of Economics and worked for Lambeth Council and the Joseph Rowntree Foundation.

Sandra Vegeris is a Senior Research Fellow at the Policy Studies Institute. She is a policy researcher and programme evaluator and has been working in policy areas relevant to lone parents for more than seven years. She is currently a member of the consortium evaluating the Employment Retention and Advancement (ERA) programme.

John Veit-Wilson is Visiting Professor in Sociology at the University of Newcastle-upon-Tyne and Emeritus Professor of Social Policy at Northumbria University. He is an Academician of Social Science and was a founding member of the Child Poverty Action Group in 1965. His proposal in 1994 of minimum income standards that are neither narrowly scientific nor merely political is now increasingly noted in the European Union as a step towards viable national criteria of income adequacy for social inclusion.

Wendy Wrapson has a background in social, health, and economic psychology. Her interest in poverty arose out of working on a study investigating consumer debt in poor households in the UK. Her other research interests include community involvement in crime prevention and the role the private security industry plays in the public's perceptions of personal safety.

Asghar Zaidi is a Senior Economist at the Social Policy Division, OECD, Paris and he is also Director of Research at the European Centre in Vienna. At OECD he is working on issues related to pension policy in OECD countries. In the past he worked as an Economic Adviser at the UK government's Department for Work and Pensions, and as a researcher at the Social Policy Department of the London School of Economics and the University of Oxford.

Foreword

I never fail to be shocked by the attempts of some of those in the media, and elsewhere, to glamourise poverty. As anyone who has ever lived with it knows, there is nothing romantic, simple or desirable about the reality – and one of the most important things that this book does is bring that reality to life. The voices of ordinary people living in 21st century Britain jump off the pages that follow, with their vivid descriptions of what their lives are actually like and the stress, misery and ill-health that their poverty causes.

We are, however, a long way from the massive unemployment and rising poverty of the 1980s and 90s. The changes that took place then were so catastrophic for so many aspects of so many lives, not least those of children who suffered the effects in their education, housing and longer-term life chances. Poverty of income and opportunity lowered and blocked the aspirations of many and led to a downward spiral of hopelessness and long term reliance on state support. Unlike in 1997, Britain today is no longer carrying that shameful mantle of the worst child poverty rates in Europe – instead we are improving fastest. This book identifies the important changes in the political debate that have taken place in the last 10 years, for example, there is no longer a discussion as to whether we should tackle child poverty but, rather, how – and how quickly.

Yet, it interested me that so many thousands of people were (rightly) willing to show their support for tackling poverty in the developing world through the Make Poverty History campaign – and still the situation here at home provokes rather less public passion. This book provides a timely reality check in exposing the many and complex issues that remain because money does, of course, matter. This point is graphically emphasised by the poverty premium, which means that there is an additional cost for poor people simply to pay for their gas and electricity and, as many of the groups that I have been working with on social fund reform over the last 18 months have pointed out, for accessing credit in times of necessity.

This publication is honest in saying that there is no silver bullet to tackle the lack of resources experienced by some families. If we are truly going to ensure that all children live in homes where there is no struggle to make ends meet then a long-term, sustainable approach is needed.

It is time for all sections of society to come together on this – government and politicians, of course, but also people living in poverty and those who say they care, as well as employers, service-providers and organisations at all levels across the public, private and voluntary sectors.

We have travelled far in the last decade through rising levels of employment, welfare-to-work initiatives and the introduction of tax credits alongside the national minimum wage. But there is a long road ahead if we are to ensure that benefits and the modern welfare state are not a trap, but rather a trampoline that enables mutuality and interdependence to demonstrate caring in practice.

David Blunkett

Rt Hon David Blunkett MP

Acknowledgements

We would like to thank all the authors for so generously giving their expertise and their energies to this volume. They are leaders in their respective fields and the campaign to end child poverty benefits greatly from the high quality of their research and analysis.

We are very grateful to the parents in the discussion at ATD Fourth World for sharing their personal stories. We hope their experiences are well reflected and that they underpin the analysis throughout. We would also like to thank ATD Fourth World for organising the session.

We really appreciate the work of Ravi Wickremasinghe in putting together the final volume and to Ben Dempsey, Phillipa Hunt, Carol Lever, Claire Walker and Munira Wilson for all their work to ensure it has an impact on policy, and in turn on the lives of children.

Save the Children is hugely grateful to Ruth Lister for co-editing this volume. Her support has been invaluable in making this book happen.

We hope this volume goes some small way to championing "the right of every child to a standard of living adequate for the child's physical, mental, spiritual, moral and social development" as enshrined in Article 27 of the United Nations Convention on the Rights of the Child, and to ensuring that right is realised.

Introduction

Jason Strelitz and Ruth Lister

Does money matter? More than at any time in recent years, this question is central to policy debates. One such debate is concerned with whether the continued pursuit of a more affluent society and personal wealth enhances our collective and individual happiness and wellbeing.

A different debate is focused on the least well off in our society and is at the heart of a political concern over how to eradicate child poverty in the UK: to what extent is supporting the incomes of families living in poverty fundamental to achieving this goal?

These two debates are linked. There is significant evidence that 'above a certain level' of income, money doesn't really matter; it doesn't buy that much more happiness or contentment.[1] This has increasingly led people to question how policy can support those things that 'really do matter'. Yet the other conclusion from the present work is that 'below a certain level', money really does matter. If people don't have enough to afford the basics, to provide what is needed in a society to do more than just get by, shortages of money really affect people's lives and stunt their capacity to flourish.

Poverty, by its definition, refers to a lack of sufficient material resources. Yet in the UK, agreement tends to end there. For some, the idea that there is real child poverty in the UK is anathema, when pictures of 'helpless' African children appear on our televisions, or when material living standards in the UK have risen so palpably in recent decades.[2] For many others, who accept the existence of poverty in the UK, it is perceived to be the result of problematic behaviours and values, and solutions therefore lie in addressing those behaviours.[3] A third perspective is that poverty does exist, and central to the experience of living in poverty is a lack of income. Poverty is associated with many negative experiences and outcomes, and a shortage of financial resources is seen as being at the root of many of those. This is the view of Save the Children and that of more than 100 organisations behind the Campaign to

End Child Poverty in the UK, a campaign that brings together many children's charities, trade unions and other organisations concerned with the rights, welfare and life chances of the UK's children.

The present Labour government set a ground-breaking target in 1999, when it pledged to eradicate child poverty by 2020. It set an interim target of halving child poverty by 2010. It measures poverty by the standard used in most Organisation for Economic Co-operation and Development (OECD) countries: poverty is living in a household with an income below 60% median. For all its limitations, this method of measurement rightly embeds a notion of relative poverty in government policy and in political debate.[4]

The terms of that debate have shifted completely. All major political parties are committed to the goal of eradicating child poverty. The Conservative Party, which for so long denied the existence of poverty in the UK, now accepts its relative nature. As David Cameron has said:

> *"We need to think of poverty in relative terms – the fact that some people lack those things which others in society take for granted… in the next 25 years, I want my Party to be in the vanguard of the fight against poverty…"*
>
> (David Cameron, November 2006, Scarman Lecture)

Yet although there is consensus among parties about the problem, this is not the case with regard to solutions. Here, politicians' differing views reflect the wide range of opinions in the press and among the public at large about both the nature of poverty and how it should be tackled. In 2006 the Joseph Rowntree Foundation published a report arguing that £4.5 billion of targeted annual investment in income-boosting measures would be needed to meet the target of halving child poverty by 2010. This figure has been taken on by those campaigning to end child poverty. It has brought to the forefront of the debate the questions: to what extent is poverty successfully tackled by raising people's incomes? To what extent does it require something else? Few fully reject either of the propositions that lie behind these questions; it is the relative balance that is up for debate. Those sceptical of further support for incomes as a key policy tool tend to say that benefits and tax credits have gone far enough. The idea is put forward that poverty is about more than money, and this leads to the marginalisation of the question of income, and a focus instead on other issues. This thinking is driven by a number of concerns.

First, there is the belief held by some, as mentioned previously, that poverty doesn't really exist in the UK. This is partly predicated on historical and cross-national comparison, and partly based on a misunderstanding of the levels of income that people live on and their actual purchasing power in the UK today.

For some, concern with child poverty is less about the poverty that children actually experience (their right to a decent standard of living), and more about its perceived negative impact on their life chances. Child poverty is seen to undermine meritocracy or equality of opportunity, and is either unjust or inefficient, depending on your perspective. But, the logic may continue, if our concern is with life chances, then surely these are affected mostly by people's ability to participate effectively in the labour market and, in the 21st century, this means the level of skills and capabilities that they have. In turn, this might suggest that policy should focus on early years, education and skills development, or indeed on the quality of role models that young people have, and particularly on whether or not their parents are in work.

The capabilities approach, on which such arguments sometimes draw, is concerned with the end of what people are able to be and do rather than with incomes, which, it is argued, are simply a means to that end. Although a focus on capabilities does not necessarily mean discounting the significance of money entirely, some commentators have contended that it points to prioritising investment in education and skills over raising incomes.

Another concern is that 'poor families' do not use resources responsibly, the perception being that parents waste money on 'booze and fags'. This means that they already have enough money (if only they spent it more wisely), or that they shouldn't have any extra money because it will only be wasted. For those concerned with child poverty, the conclusion is therefore that resources should be focused on public goods, such as health and education, which can improve the lives of children, regardless of their parents' 'fecklessness'.

Connected to this idea is the notion that poverty, rather than being about a lack of resources, is the consequence and embodiment of a particular range of behaviours, values and aspirations. This is what is sometimes described as the 'culture of poverty', characteristic of the 'underclass'. People in the UK are more likely than those in most European countries to ascribe poverty to people's own laziness and lack of will-power. If we conclude this, we are unlikely to think that supporting family incomes is part of the solution; indeed, advocates of this view are more likely to believe that supporting incomes is a part of the problem, allowing people to become dependent and demotivating them from 'pulling themselves up by their bootstraps'. Today, politicians frequently talk about poverty of aspirations as being equally important as poverty of income, without regard to the evidence that parents and children living in poverty often have very real aspirations but lack the material means to realise them.[5]

Each of these positions enjoys support among the general public. Yet the evidence presented in this volume points strongly to the need to support family incomes to a far greater extent if we are to be able to eradicate child poverty once and for all. Low income affects every aspect of families' and children's lives, from their health, housing and education to the wellbeing of the family, through the impact of debt and the psychological impact of the struggle to make ends meet. Low income lowers children's standard of living well below what most people would deem an acceptable level for a country of the UK's wealth. Moreover, low income has a direct impact on children's life chances as well, affecting their cognitive and behavioural development.

The evidence in this book shows that families on low incomes typically manage their money well and as responsibly as anyone else. When their incomes increase, they spend their resources on children's necessities and the building blocks of family life. So the tools available to government to support incomes through tax, benefits and wage policy are vital tools in improving children's lives.

In order to demonstrate 'why money matters' in the fight against child poverty, this report brings together a range of evidence. Although the evidence collected here is not comprehensive – income feeds through health, housing and neighborhoods, for example, which are not covered here – it nevertheless demonstrates powerfully the impact of low income on families' lives.

- The first piece of evidence comes directly from parents living in poverty themselves. They speak out about the impact of low incomes on their lives and their children's lives. (Chapter 1)

Part I: Poverty – its material impact and costs

- Despite free schooling, education costs money in various ways and poverty has a direct impact within the school gates, affecting children's experience of schooling and their *education*. (Chapter 2)
- While our standard measures of poverty reflect household size and age, they do not account for *disability*. However, households where people have

disabilities *face extra costs*, and while these are unaccounted for there will remain a hidden poverty. (Chapter 3)

- Diets are critical to children's *health and development*, and there is a direct relationship between families' income and the provision of a nutritious *diet* for their children. (Chapter 4)

- *Work* is often cited as the best route out of poverty, but what are the implications of this for lone parents, who are likely to have few qualifications and to need flexible hours so they can care for their children? In these circumstances the labour market does not necessarily provide that route, and may come with significant costs, both financial and family related. (Chapter 5)

- Persistent lack of income leads to *debt*. This exacerbates the problems experienced by families in poverty, with the impact of servicing debts on household incomes and on anxiety and stress. (Chapter 6)

- People in poverty pay more for purchasing essential goods and services, and face a *poverty premium* when paying for gas and electricity or borrowing money, which means that a family in poverty may spend an extra £1,000 per year on these items compared with a more affluent family. (Chapter 7)

Part II: Poverty – its impact on wellbeing

- It is widely accepted that *early child development* is a vital precursor of later life chances, and incomes have a very strong impact on early health, behavioural and cognitive development. (Chapter 8)

- Poverty has a major *psychological impact*, affecting people's view of their lives both day to day and in the longer term. (Chapter 9)

- To live in poverty in the UK is to be stigmatised, and the result for many individuals is feelings of *shame and lack of a sense of worth*. Policy can mitigate this but too often in reality exacerbates it. (Chapter 10)

- *"Time is the ultimate scarce resource"* but use of time, our ability to generate resources, consume and care are all affected by the material resources we have. (Chapter 11)

Part III: Ensuring a decent income for all

- Poverty is about the inability to meet the *cost of necessities*, and yet the way we choose to support different individuals' incomes in no way reflects even the cost of the most basic necessities. (Chapter 12)

- The increases that low-income families have received in recent years have largely been *spent to the benefit of their children*. While different households manage their finances differently, parents (especially mothers) protect their children from poverty as much as possible at their own expense. (Chapter 13)
- If our goal is a society free from poverty, then policies that support people's incomes through the tax and benefit system ought to be underpinned by notions of *'adequacy'*. (Chapter 14)
- At the heart of a sustainable approach to tackling poverty is ensuring *decent wages* for all, which can provide for an adequate standard of living, and give people the dignity of earning and supporting themselves and their families. (Chapter 15)

The volume concludes by bringing out the core messages of these chapters:

- Money matters. It underpins so much of the experience of families struggling to get by on a low income.
- As low-income families' incomes increase, so outcomes improve; children's lives in particular are enhanced.
- The government's commitment to ending child poverty must be supported by a set of policies which, over the long term, ensure that those both in and outside work have sufficient incomes to provide for themselves and their families at a level that enables them to live with decency and with their dignity respected.

Notes

[1] R Layard, *Happiness: lessons for a new science*, Penguin, London, 2006.

[2] A Alexander, 'Cameron has fallen into the poverty trap', *Daily Mail*, 1 December 2006.

[3] C Murray, *Underclass + 10*, Civitas, [London?] 2001.

[4] The government does use other indicators of poverty, such as persistent income poverty and a combined income and deprivation indicator, although the debate focuses very strongly on the annual statistics on incomes below 60% median.

[5] P Seaman, K Turner, M Hill, A Stafford, M Walker, *Parenting and Children's Resilience in Disadvantaged Communities*, National Children's Bureau, London, 2005.

1 'Everyone needs money': the voices of parents who have too little

Ruth Lister and Jason Strelitz

A small group of parents with experience of poverty gave their views on why and how money matters during a focus group discussion carried out in the summer of 2007 with the assistance of ATD Fourth World (see Chapter 10). Three mothers (Anne, Dawn and Kelly) participated in the whole discussion; Chandra arrived in the middle and Tina and Tony towards the end.[1] The discussion covered both general questions about the significance of money and more specific implications of not having enough money. Extracts from the discussion are reproduced here with minimal commentary because we believe that what the participants had to say provides a powerful insight into why money matters. We are very grateful to them for giving us their time.

Getting by under pressure

Much of the conversation centred on the difficulties of getting by on insufficient money. The extracts illustrate Fran Bennett's point in Chapter 13 about the "tenacity and determination needed just to keep going". This came across very clearly as we listened to the mothers talking about their everyday lives.

> *My second son Tom has got special needs. I am under pressure; they are looking for the latest jeans and I do get under pressure because I can't afford them. I would love to be able to put the kids in more clubs and for them to join things, but at the present time I can't do it. I try to bring them to the park and do things, you know, and they are looking for football kits and things like that, but I just can't do it.* (Dawn)

I just look for the cheapest things really. You know that's what makes my money last longer, and that's how I can buy a few bits and bobs for my daughter. If I've got money left over, then I just save it in my bank… (Kelly)

It's trying to stay in control of everything – the children, the school, it's just everything. Family's just hard. And trying to give them a good possible start. Because what you put in now is for later, you know. It's what you sow you reap. (Dawn)

I try not to get into debt. My kids have asked me to get a catalogue, but I'd never do a catalogue because I worry about getting in debt. My eldest one said 'if we get a catalogue, I can order whatever I like'. I told him, I would rather pay cash down, then I know it's yours. I worry because I might be paying the catalogue and I might not be able to afford it. I just worry about that panic. (Dawn)

Before I was pregnant I didn't know the value of money. And now I know that a pound can last a long time if you think about it. You can get milk and bread and even butter with a pound. If you don't know how to spend it wisely, then when you get your own flat you never know how the money's going to last you. You've got to pay rent, provide for your own children… (Kelly)

As the children grow up, they need more of everything, they're eating more, clothes… I think it really takes £100 to keep a child for a week not £30. To be able to feed them properly, especially when they're 13, because they do eat a lot. A lot. If you don't feed them properly then they'll be miserable, very miserable. I always believe in the feeding. Because if they are not fed properly they will be irritable. (Dawn)

It's very hard saving on low income. It's very hard to put money aside because now that the children are getting older they need something all the time; either underwear or a t-shirt or skirt, children are always needing something. It is very hard to put money away. I don't really put money away to be honest. (Dawn)

Tax credits: additional pressure

Unfortunately, tax credits, which were designed to help low-income families, were talked about as a source of additional pressure because of the effects of the repayment of over-payments. It was the first matter that Anne raised and she returned to it during the discussion because it was clearly preoccupying her and putting her under considerable strain.

I was just saying about the family tax credit: most people I know have been affected by it. If you went to a shop and they had a certain price for something, say like three pounds, and they'd mis-priced it, then you'd just pay it. You wouldn't be expected to go away and get a letter saying we mis-priced it, can you come back and pay it. And that's what's happening to our families. It is affecting our families a great deal. I think the government should recognise they've made a big error with that, and that it's their fault. (Anne)

I was really upset. I cried. I couldn't believe it at first. Now I'm just resigned to it. Okay then, take the money back. It's just really upsetting. Very upsetting. When a bill comes in it's very hard. (Anne)

Yeah, they make an error and then you're left to pick up the pieces. You think you can carry on with your life as normal and then they start deducting money from your money. They don't set a rate, they just say we're taking this much a week blah blah blah and they start taking it. At the end of the day, you found it hard enough to live on what you had in the first place, so how can you start taking less away. It just means you've got less to work with. It's a lot harder. (Tony)

Paying the price or going without

A common refrain was the high costs associated with education (discussed in Chapter 2). Furnishing accommodation and coping with broken equipment were other problems raised to illustrate the difficulties of managing on a low income.

Yes because they need to have a jumper with the logo on it. Well, you don't have to, they can wear the plain blue ones, but that's £9 for the jumper and the t-shirts are £6.50 with a logo on them as well. Sometimes I just get the plain blue ones or the plain white ones at the market. I'd say the average for one primary school kid is about £100 per uniform, maybe £80 to £100 roughly. (Dawn)

[Others in room agree.]

And then a secondary school kid is a lot more. I have a secondary school kid as well, which comes to about £200 to £300, secondary school uniform. With the shoes, as I said he's a size ten, and he's very tall – he's five foot ten. So… (Dawn)

At the school recently, they've had trips which were £15 for the little ones. They went to a farm and then the years three to six went to the seaside, which was

£10 each, plus they needed some spending money. That was quite a large sum – £35 for the three. And I had to give Tom some money, a bit of spending money. (Kelly)

I do have one laptop. I got it from PC World. I've been paying off £8 a week. But in total it's come to nearly £952, just for the laptop. I've nearly paid it off now. He needed a laptop for school you see, my son the eldest one. He is nearly 14. I don't want to keep begging off my brother. (Dawn)

[Do you know how much it would have cost to buy outright?]

I could have got one for £400. (Dawn)

Accommodation… there is nothing: no fridge, no cooker, no washing machine, no bed, no carpet… so how can I manage? It's very difficult. (Chandra)

If my washing machine breaks down, I can't afford to keep going to the launderette. (Tina)

When I first ever moved into my flat I had nothing. And all the social gave me was £100 – that was like to get furniture. And I'm like how the hell am I meant to do this on £100! So I had to go to Shaftesbury's. If it weren't for Shaftesbury's I wouldn't have had no furniture in my house. £100 they gave me. And I was so upset about that. (Tina)

Impact on children

The conversation constantly came back to children – how they miss out and how they are treated by other children. Parents were acutely aware of the stigma their children can face at school: one example of how public services can exacerbate poverty's impact is discussed by Matt Davies in Chapter 10.

They're entitled to a free packed lunch, but they won't take a free packed lunch because they're too embarrassed. They won't take a packed lunch at the school. They'll get teased, they want to go along with the others. But I don't mind doing that really. (Dawn)

They would rather they come home because they get teased. They get very embarrassed. And they come home and have a go at me. Why did I let them take a school lunch? They are aware of that at nine, ten years. They are very aware. They get very embarrassed if they have one that the school provides, they'd rather have one that I make. They just don't want to go and get a school lunch. They'd get bullied and teased for weeks after. Because the kids told me before: they watch who goes and gets the school lunch and then they bully them. It's very hard for them, it's very hard. (Dawn)

It's that once you get your money, once your bills are paid – your gas, your electric, your rent – you sit there and think, oh, I've got everything I need but I can't do anything with the kids because there's nowhere to take them. So they miss out. All right you can take them to a park, it don't cost you nothing, but then when they get a bit older, they're not interested in parks no more. They want to go to farms, go to this, go to there, and you're like I haven't got the money. It is a struggle. It's a struggle for us. (Tina)

Although I've got my electric and my food, but say it's a nice weekend, I can't take the kids anywhere because I've only got a fiver. Where can I take them on a fiver? (Tina)

At the moment, I've got two kids sleeping in a single bed. I haven't got a bunk bed. And I'm scrimping and scraping to get the money together to get a bunk bed because I don't want them in a single bed together for the rest of their lives. (Tina)

And also when the kids are growing up, if the parents can't buy them the latest things. Then you also get like an occurrence of bullying: ah, look at your trainers, ah, look at your clothes – you're a tramp. (Tony)

Children: ambitions and putting them first

We asked a specific question about the parents' hopes for themselves and their children. Again, they tended to focus on the children. This reflected a recurrent theme of putting children first, which once more exemplified the arguments in Fran Bennett's chapter.

I hope they don't get involved in crime. I hope they learn to be individuals. I'd like them to travel. I'd always wished that I'd travelled, that's my one regret – I really would've liked to have travelled more. I hope they travel. I think it's very important to travel to see different ways of life and to appreciate what you've got. I just want them to be happy. (Anne)

I think they become a good citizen... you know a good education... they will be good children... with no problem in the future. (Chandra)

I'd feel happy if I had more money. The bills do get paid but sometimes they take a little bit longer and it would be nice to be able to pay things and just give the kids a better quality of life. To take them more interesting places. (Anne)

I am not wish a lot of money, but I wish I spend a good life, like you know if my child wish anything then I provide. I try and give them everything they wish. (Chandra)

I can't buy myself something that's really unusual. You do make a lot of sacrifices, you try and put the kids first. We go without to give to the children. (Dawn)

People in general, if they had more money then they wouldn't be as stressed. You do worry when you've got children. The rich and poor worry about their children I suppose, because you're not really number one, your children are number one. They're the most important thing in your life. (Dawn)

Impact on parents

Putting children first takes its toll on parents both physically and mentally.

At the end of the day, you end up going without, under-nourishing yourself. Obviously you under-nourish yourself because you never under-nourish your children. It ends up making you ill, and what happens to your children when you're ill? You just have to get on with it. It makes it harder. (Tony)

You get quite isolated sometimes if you haven't got a lot of money. You can't do things, so you stay indoors and watch a lot of television. And then there's adverts on the television, like 'if you owe this amount of money…' and you think, God, please leave me alone, I don't need to be reminded of my situation at the moment. It's just hard you know: you stay in because you've not got any money, and then there's rubbish on the television so sometimes you just get really depressed about it. It's just frustrating sometimes, very frustrating. (Anne)

Yeah sometimes. I'm not really an envious person but then sometimes… I know my life will improve when they get a bit older, but you just think 'why can't I have that' sometimes. It does get very hard. Sometimes you're okay but then other times you get very low about it. You don't want to go out and it's an effort to say hello to people sometimes because you're feeling so low. But then other days you're all right. (Anne)

Yeah. Sometimes. If I feel quite low, I hope the kids don't pick up on it but I'm sure they do sometimes. My daughter will say 'come on Mum, give me a smile' and I think oh no. Your partner comes home and you're watching the telly and you're like 'why can't we go out', you know. You work six days and on Sunday you want to go somewhere other than the park. (Anne)

I live in rented accommodation, I'd like to live in a house but the pricing of the houses... I couldn't afford the house when I was working and, going back part-time, I won't be able to anyway. So things like that make me quite upset. I've never had a garden. I'd like my kids to have a garden. Sometimes you really get disheartened. I'm sure I'll be okay. They are regenerating the area... and it's just the houses prices... how are people supposed to improve their lives when they can't afford to buy a house? It's very hard. (Anne)

My big girl, when she asks, 'I need something' and I can't provide, I'm very upset. (Chandra)

Work and care

The mothers talked about the competing responsibilities of going back to work and caring for their children themselves. They illustrate Lesley Hoggart and Sandra Vegeris' conclusion in Chapter 5 that "lone parents' decisions about work are not taken without considering their children".

I'm on benefits. I'm on me own. I bring up four children. I split up with their dad. I would love to work, but I'm glad to run the household and pick up the four kids. (Dawn)

I would like to go back to work on a part-time basis. I'd like to work in a school, maybe as a teaching assistant, to fit in with the children's holidays. (Anne)

I think they should treat people individually... It should be recognised that if a mother wants to stay at home and look after her children, then she should be able to do so. Financially she should be encouraged to do that, not be forced to work, leaving her children. It's hard enough looking after children, let alone coming home and looking after children. I worked for at least eight years... I sometimes feel like we're being penalised because I don't want to work yet because my children are young. (Anne)

But I will work when the kids are old enough to leave home, do whatever, then I will go to work but until then I've got children to look after. I brought them into the world, it's my responsibility to look after them. (Tina)

I don't have a job because I look after the children, you know I tried but it's very difficult. How can I manage because the smallest is two years? How can I manage them and pay the bills? (Chandra)

Why money matters

We started and ended the discussion with a direct question about why money matters and what message we should be stressing in this volume. While initial responses tended to focus on the practical difficulties of getting by, the participants were also very clear about the fact that money does matter and why it matters.

Because I know money doesn't make you happy, but you need a certain amount of money to make you happy and comfortable as well. When you've got children, you need to take them out every so often to keep them happy as well, especially when you are stuck in flats. (Dawn)

When you haven't got a lot of money, you feel more deprived, excluded, isolated. You feel that you're in a rut and you can't get out of because you've got no money. Having money would make a lot of people happy because you're always sort of struggling, struggling from day to day…I'm talking about all the people working in low-paid work, benefits. As I said before you feel more deprived, excluded, isolated… it all sort of comes as a package. (Dawn)

Money is an issue in everybody's life. Everyone needs money. (Anne)

Note

[1] The discussion took place at ATD Fourth World in informal surroundings and lasted about two hours. All names have been changed to preserve anonymity.

Part 1

Poverty: its material impact and costs

2 Education and child poverty

Gabrielle Preston

Despite a massive increase in government spending on education, the association between poverty and poor educational outcomes remains firmly in place. A child's experience at school is dictated by family income. While recent research suggests that the government, local authorities and schools could and should do much more to reduce barriers to education – such as costs, selection and exclusion – educational initiatives cannot, on their own, compensate a child for the stigma and deprivation associated with being poor. Indeed, income poverty may actively undermine the impact and efficacy of the resources being poured into the educational system. The inequalities that blight the education system will not be reduced until parents are better protected from the stress and trauma associated with living with poverty, and provided with the resources they need to support their children's education, and their children are viewed as citizens with rights, rather than future employees with responsibilities.

Education and family income

While the education gap is the consequence of complex, multivariable factors that are compounded by gender, ethnicity, special educational needs, family structure and parents' level of education, there is no doubt that a child's experiences and development during the early years and at school are affected by family income. Although this chapter focuses on the difference money makes during the school years, it is difficult to separate poor children's experiences of education from the financial, health, social and cultural needs of parents, carers and families before, during and after their birth.

Research emanating from a wide spectrum of disciplines has long indicated that a child's earliest encounters with their parent/carer will have a lifelong impact on their development and their capacity to enjoy life and relate to others.[1] But for parents this can be a difficult and stressful time, particularly if they are trying to cope with the strain and stigma associated with poverty. Not only does poverty leave parents struggling to provide nutritious food, warmth and appropriate clothing for their children, but it exacts a toll on their physical and mental wellbeing. This renders 'good' parenting more difficult and, indeed, reduces the impact that positive parenting can have.[2] Meanwhile, recent research reveals "a very sharp rise in the association between educational attainment and family income".[3]

Poverty and educational exclusion

Poverty not only blights very young children's lives, but it contributes to differences in young children's cognitive and social development from a very young age. Data show that children's attainment is already structured by social class at 22 months and its impact on attainment levels gets more extreme by the age of ten.[4] More recent evidence has found that by the age of three some disadvantaged children are lagging a full year behind their better-off peer group in terms of cognitive development, social skills and school readiness.[5]

Given the above issues, it is undoubtedly the case that children from disadvantaged backgrounds arrive in mainstream education with significant problems that are hard for teachers and schools to cope with, let alone resolve. However, while it is unreasonable to expect the education system to redress profound socio-economic disadvantages, it a source of concern that, for the moment at least, it seems to be compounding them.[6] So what is going wrong?

Just as disadvantaged parents face barriers to employment, their children face barriers to education that are compounded by lack of money. Given that better schools tend to be in more affluent areas, where high house prices and expensive uniforms keep out poor children,[7] it is hardly surprising that "disadvantaged children are more likely to be attending poorly performing secondary schools".[8] The Sutton Trust reveals that the overall proportion of pupils eligible for free school meals at the 200 highest-performing comprehensive schools was 5.6% compared with 14.3% in secondary schools nationally.[9]

Furthermore, poorer children are often excluded from the educational opportunities that are available to better-off children, whatever school they attend. A recent survey found that in secondary school three-quarters of parents "found it difficult to meet the cost of school uniform… or school trips", and 71% found it "difficult to meet all the costs in the survey". Although the situation is slightly better in primary schools, the findings are still stark: "Many parents are faced with significant extra costs associated with sending their children to school. These costs vary considerably between schools and can cause difficulties for low income families." [10]

Additional costs not only have a profoundly negative impact on a child's ability to access the more creative aspects of the curriculum such as music, art, photography and some sports; they present barriers to the core curriculum. For example, poorer children may not be able to buy revision guides and educational materials within schools, or computers at home. Research undertaken by the media regulator Ofcom reveals "a stark social contrast between children from low income households who have internet access at home and those who do not". [11] The possibilities for participating in foreign trips or student exchanges are limited. Furthermore, extra costs generate stress and anxiety for both parents and children. [12] Information sent home about activities that require financial contributions may be quietly thrown away by a child intent on protecting a worried parent.

Disadvantaged children experience other barriers to getting the most out of the curriculum. Research has found that they tend to view schools as a more punitive environment than their more affluent peer group. [13] Perhaps poorer children are subjected to a curriculum that does not reflect their cultural experiences and therefore may seem pointless. [14] Maybe they are given 'undemanding staff' in the classroom or are treated as 'different' and less able than more affluent pupils. Their sense of themselves and their ambitions is constrained by an awareness of where they and their parents stand in an unequal society.

While research indicates that "almost all parents/carers of school-aged children agreed that a good education would help their child get ahead in life", [15] there is also evidence that families sometimes find it difficult to engage with schools. Although this might be due to cultural factors, or the consequence of their own unrewarding encounters with the school system, research also suggests that "parents in working-class communities had limited time and income to supplement and intervene in children's schooling". [16] However, while it is also possible that disadvantaged families and their children expect less from an educational system that does not seem to have them in mind, much more research is needed on the impact that poverty has on the expectations of policy-makers and educational practitioners themselves.

And of course a great deal of creative learning takes place outside school. However, although disadvantaged children, who tend to engage in fewer organised activities, may have more free time than their more affluent peer group,[17] they are often unable to take part in creative or stimulating activities in the wider community, many of which may be in short supply locally, and are often expensive and difficult to access.

Given the problems that disadvantaged children encounter at school and the dearth of opportunities within local communities, it is particularly important that they engage in after-school activities, especially during half-terms and holidays. However, although the government has promised that every child will be able to access breakfast clubs, out-of-hours tuition and after-school clubs in sport, music and drama,[18] and it has stipulated that local authorities must ensure that "children with disabilities or special educational needs must be able to access all the services",[19] guidance has been issued to schools that allows them to charge for extra curricula activities.[20] Other disadvantaged groups – for example, children with sick or disabled parents, who may experience high levels of social exclusion as well as poverty – are not specifically mentioned. Recent research shows that young people on free school meals are "less likely to participate in after school activities than those from more affluent homes… because rich parents were able to buy their children access to such clubs, while poorer parents could not".[21] Furthermore, children who feel alienated from the school system may be reluctant to avail themselves of extended school provision.[22]

Lack of money is associated with other barriers to education. Children from disadvantaged backgrounds are much more likely to be excluded, or to exclude themselves, from school. Research indicates that pupils' attendance "tends to be lower in schools with higher levels of socio-economic disadvantage".[23] While the reasons for this are complex, research suggests it is in part "likely to be due to higher levels of sickness".[24] This is hardly surprising, given the close connection between poverty and health problems.

A shocking number of children who face the greatest risk of poverty end up out of education, employment and training altogether, many from the age of 14.[25] Again, the reasons for this are varied and complex, but these children are more likely to report having left education "because of the need to earn money or because their parents could not afford for them to continue".[26]

To its credit, the government recognises that money is a factor. The introduction of the Educational Maintenance Allowance (EMA), payable to 16–18-year-olds from low-income families when they follow specified educational and training courses, has successfully increased participation in full-time education.[27] The Department for Children, Schools and Families (DCSF) is currently trialling an extension of EMA "to include all educational provision that is approved by local authorities... [and] to all young people taking Entry to Employment courses".[28] While additional income is always welcome, anecdotal evidence suggests that EMA may be affected by problems commonly associated with means-tested support, such as misunderstandings about entitlement, and stigma.

Furthermore, the manner in which financial support is channelled to low-income families can seem arbitrary and unjust. For example, in England free school meals are not available to low-income families who are in work, despite high levels of child poverty in working families,[29] and children in workless families – who face the greatest risk of poverty – may not be able to access childcare or extended school provision because their parent/carer is not entitled to the childcare element of working tax credit. Take-up of both free school meals and the childcare element of tax credits is very low among poorer families.[30] However, all poor children should have access to a hot midday school meal and be able to participate in extra-curricular activities irrespective of their parents' work status.

There are other problems with ways in which the limited financial support that is available is channelled to families. The provision of discretionary support from local authorities – for example, school uniform grants and clothing grants – generates 'postcode lotteries' and confusion. Accessing and utilising such grants is, in any case, both stigmatising and inflexible. Furthermore, complex funding streams within local authorities and schools sometimes prevent money getting to the children who need it most.[31]

Conclusion

While the money and support that is being channelled into the education system by the government is very welcome, it does not mean that money – or choice – is put in the hands of poorer families. In fact, the discrepancy between investment in educational support and improvements in educational experiences of poor children strongly suggests that income poverty is actively undermining the impact that expensive educational initiatives could have on the lives of poor children.

Research suggests that a radically different approach is needed. However, there are few signs that this is in the offing. The government is continuing to focus on paid employment to increase incomes, and education to compensate children for a difficult and damaging start in life. Although the government argues that this two-pronged approach constitutes a coherent strategy on child poverty there is ample evidence that it is not sufficient. Research shows that poorer families are less likely to access – and often get a worse deal out of – health and education services than better-off families, and that if they do move into employment, they are more likely to get low-paid, part-time jobs that do nothing to reduce child poverty.

Meanwhile, policies that are dictated more by a parent's work status than a child's needs have eclipsed a more child-focused approach to parenting, childcare and education. The emphasis on paid employment rather than benefit adequacy to safeguard families from poverty is damaging children in workless households. Recent research indicates that some government initiatives to support working families – such as the extension of childcare, after-school clubs and educational activities – have significantly *increased* the cost of bringing up a child.[32] This does not bode well for parents who are living in poverty.

While the publication of the DCSF's Children's Plan is a very welcome recognition of the importance of a more holistic approach, based on the needs of children and families, it remains to be seen whether funding and staffing levels will prove adequate, or whether disparate services will be capable of co-operating effectively. The government's failure as yet to implement a 'joined-up' approach to children, and the gap between aspirational and often enlightened rhetoric and actual outcomes, have long been a cause of concern.

If the government is to succeed in improving childhood experiences and outcomes for children, then it must deliver policies across all departments that put children first. And so, while improving the school environment, reviewing the curriculum and methods of teaching and putting more holistic support services in place are clearly important, increasing income for prospective parents and families is crucial to maximise children's wellbeing and happiness during the school years. Increasing family income is the most effective way of targeting resources on disadvantaged children.

Notes

[1] See, for example, Isobel E P Menzies, 'Thoughts on the maternal role in contemporary society', *Child Psychotherapy*, 4:1, 1975, which reports: "Such views appear to have been incontrovertibly established by a mass of research." (p. 10).

[2] L Feinstein, B Hearn and Z Renton with C Abrahams and M MacLeod, *Reducing Inequalities: Realising the talents of all*, National Children's Bureau, Family and Parenting Institute, Institute of Education, London, 2007, p. 18.

[3] J Blanden and S Machin, *Recent Changes in Intergenerational Mobility in Britain*, report for Sutton Trust, December 2007, p. 19.

[4] L Feinstein, 'Inequality in the Early Cognitive Development of British Children in the 1970 cohort', *Economica*, 70, pp. 73–97.

[5] Kirstine Hansen and Heather Joshi (eds) *Millennium Cohort Study Second Survey: A user's guide to initial findings*, Centre for Longitudinal Studies, Institute of Education, University of London, 2007.

[6] See Robert Cassen and Geeta Gindon, *Tackling Low Educational Achievement*, Joseph Rowntree Foundation, 2007, p. 25.

[7] *Adding Up: The range and impact of school costs on families* (Barnardo's, CPAG, Citizens' Advice Bureau, End Child Poverty, Family Welfare Association, National Union of Teachers, One Parent Families/Gingerbread, Save the Children, 2007) reveals "little compliance with the principles of the [School Admissions Code] by the schools represented in the survey".

[8] See Robert Cassen and Geeta Gindon, *Tackling Low Educational Achievement*, Joseph Rowntree Foundation, 2007.

[9] Sutton Trust, *The Social Composition of Top Comprehensive Schools: Rates of eligibility for free school meals at the 200 highest performing comprehensive schools*, Sutton Trust, January 2006.

[10] School Cost Coalition, *Adding Up: The range and impact of school costs on families*, School Cost Coalition, September 2007.

[11] Ofcom, *Children and the Internet: A research study into the social effects of lack of internet access on socially disadvantaged children and families*, Ofcom, June 2007.

[12] See, for example, Sarah Gorin, Claire Dyson, Carol-Ann Hooper and Christie Cabral, *Living with Hardship 24/7: The diverse experiences of families living in poverty in England*, Frank Buttle Trust, 2007.

[13] See Liz Sutton, Noel Smith, Chris Dearden and Sue Middleton, *A Child's-eye View of Social Difference*, Joseph Rowntree Foundation, 2007.

[14] See Cassen and Gindon, note 8.

[15] Research reported by A West, in 'Poverty and educational achievement: why do children from low-income families tend to do less well at school?' in *Benefits: The journal of poverty and social justice*, October 2007, 15:3, p. 290.

[16] Research reported by A West; see note 15.

[17] See Sutton *et al*, note 13.

[18] See 'Extended schools – £1billion boost', Department for Children, Schools and Families (National), 25 July 2007, press release can be downloaded at: http://www.dfes.gov.uk/pns/DisplayPN.cgi?pn_id=2007_0140

[19] 'PSA Delivery Agreement 9: Halve the number of children in poverty by 2010–11, on the way to eradicating child poverty by 2020', HM Government, October 2007, p. 11. This report can be downloaded from: http://www.hm-treasury.gov.uk/media/B/9/pbr_csr07_psa9.pdf

[20] Department for Education and Skills, *Extended Schools: Access to opportunities and services for all: A prospectus*, The Stationery Office, 2006.

[21] BBC News, 11 December 2007, 'Poor "shut out by school clubs"' (available at: http://news.bbc.co.uk/1/hi/education/7138395.stm), quoting *After the Bell: Out of school hours activities for children and young people*, New Philanthropy Capital, 2007.

[22] See Sutton *et al*, note 13.

[23] A West, 'Poverty and educational achievement: why do children from low-income families tend to do less well at school?' in *Benefits: The journal of poverty and social justice*, 15:3 (October 2007), p. 288.

[24] West, p. 288 (see note 23).

[25] Recent Office of National Statistics information indicates: "The proportion of 16 and 17 year olds NEET [not in education, employment or training] has fallen from 9.5 per cent to 8.0 per cent" but "The proportion of 18 year olds NEET has risen from 13.6 per cent to 14.8 per cent".

[26] West, 2007, p. 284 (see note 23).

[27] West, 2007, p.290 (see note 23).

[28] See DCSF press release, 5 November 2007, which announced: "Children, Schools and Families Secretary Ed Balls today set out the building blocks that will underpin Government plans to raise the education participation age to 17 by 2013 and 18 by 2015".

[29] See Murray Hall Community Trust, *Join Us for Lunch: Sandwell's prepaid meals campaign – a pilot project aimed at increasing the registration of free school meals*, Murray Hall Community Trust, March 2006.

[30] R Chote, C Emmerson, D Miles and Z Oldfield, *The IFS Green Budget: January 2005*, Institute for Fiscal Studies, 2005.

[31] See, for example, Department for Education and Skills and HM Treasury, *Child Poverty: Fair funding for schools - a review of the ways in which local authorities fund schools to meet the costs arising from social deprivation amongst their pupils*, DfES, HM Treasury, 2005 (can be downloaded from: http://www.teachernet.gov.uk/_doc/9404/ACF9795.doc).

[32] The Victoria Liverpool Friendly Society's annual 'Cost of a Child' survey, now in its fourth year, shows that the cost of bringing up a child in 2007 is 9% higher than the previous year; the cost of raising a child has increased by 33% over the five years since the survey began in 2003. Childcare and education remain the biggest expenditures, costing parents £50,538 and £47,310. See www.lv.com/media_centre/press_releases/cost

3 Disabled children, poverty and extra costs

Tania Burchardt and Asghar Zaidi

Introduction

Official statistics show that children in families affected by disability are at considerably higher risk of poverty. Among the 3.2 million children in families with a disabled adult and/or a disabled child, the proportion living below the poverty line – here defined as 60% of median income before housing costs – was 28% in 2005/06. This compares with 20% of children in families not directly affected by disability.[1]

These figures are shocking enough. But they represent an *under*estimate of the true extent of relative disadvantage experienced by these families, because the cost of living for many of them is higher than for families not affected by disability, because of additional expenses incurred in managing the child's or parent's impairments. Direct extra costs include special aids, adaptations and therapies not provided by the NHS or social services; less direct costs include additional transport, clothing, heating, food, childcare and safety measures that may be required. This means that a given income goes less far in securing a decent standard of living for the family: either the needs of the disabled person go unmet, or income is diverted to pay for these disability-related goods and services, which is then not available to pay for day-to-day living. The official statistics quoted above include disability-related benefits as income, but make no allowance for the higher cost of living for families affected by disability. Consequently, they represent an underestimate of disadvantage.

Gabrielle Preston's research on families with disabled children has provided important insights into the ways in which social security benefits designed to help with the extra costs of disability are used.[2] Preston found that receipt of

Disability Living Allowance (DLA) in some cases made the difference between social exclusion and inclusion, not only supporting the disabled child's health and development, but facilitating activities, outings and social interactions for the whole family that had previously been impossible. Unfortunately, the research also highlighted the restrictive eligibility conditions for DLA for children, and a number of barriers to take-up of entitlement, including bureaucratic hurdles and lack of 'joining up' between schools, health and social services and benefit agencies. The result is that many families in need receive no benefits at all, and among those who do the amounts are often insufficient to cover the extra costs they incur.

In this chapter, we endeavour to quantify the extra costs associated with having a disabled child in the household and to show what effect taking these extra costs into account has on estimates of child poverty. We use a method first developed by Richard Berthoud and colleagues[3] and subsequently used to estimate equivalence scales for disabled adults.[4] This 'standard of living method' is explained in the next section. It is the first time it has been applied to calculating the extra costs of disabled children.

Two other methods have previously been used to estimate the extra costs of disability for children. The 'budget standards approach' engaged a group of parents of severely disabled children in a deliberative process to work out what they regarded as the minimum necessary to bring up a child with severe disability.[5] This was then compared with the results of a previous exercise with parents of non-disabled children. The difference worked out to be £119 per week (in 2004/05 prices for comparison with the results below; this is equivalent to £132 in 2007 prices).[6]

In another study, a sample of 182 parents of severely disabled children kept expenditure diaries recording their actual spending on their children.[7] Again, these were compared with similar data collected from parents of non-disabled children. The difference was £38 per week (in 2004/05 prices; equivalent to £42 in 2007 prices). This is much lower than the difference in the budget standards identified by parents of disabled and non-disabled children, suggesting that there are many items which parents of disabled children believe are essential – and hence are included in the budget standard – but which they are unable to afford.

Methods

The reasoning behind the method used here is that to obtain the same standard of living, different families need different amounts of income because of differences in the costs they face. We cannot observe standard of living directly but we can use various indicators that are positively associated with disposable income but that are not closely connected to disability itself. Here we use the ability to make regular savings as an indicator.[8] The average difference in income required by a family with a disabled child and an otherwise similar family without a disabled child to obtain the same standard of living can be taken as an estimate of the extra costs faced by the family with a disabled child.

The calculations are made separately for single-parent and two-parent households, to avoid confusing the disability effect with other differences in household composition. In addition, we control for number of children, housing tenure, and geographical region – all of which have been found in previous work to be significant factors in the relationship between income and standard of living.

The data we use are from the Family Resources Survey for the financial year 2004/05. This is a nationally representative survey run by the Office for National Statistics of the household population of the UK. Income is defined as total disposable income before housing costs. The definition of disability, for both children and adults, is a long-standing illness or disability that limits day-to-day activities. Unfortunately, the survey does not contain further information on the severity of the limitation, so the results necessarily reflect the average. This will tend to mean that the results underestimate extra costs for families containing children with more complex needs, and overestimate extra costs for children with less severe impairments.

The results: extra costs and poverty

The standard of living method suggests that the extra costs of disability are *proportionate* to income, rather than being a fixed sum of money for rich and poor families alike. In Table 1 we therefore give the extra costs estimated as a percentage of income and, as an illustration, the equivalent amount for a family on average (mean) income.

Table 1: Extra costs of disability for families with one or more disabled children

	Extra costs as % of income	Extra costs at mean income in 2004/05 prices	Number of individuals included in estimation
Lone-parent families	18.4	£62 per week	5,647
Two-parent families	10.0	£74 per week	21,532

Note: Mean income for each family type, in 2004/05 prices; regression results available from authors on request.

Source: Family Resources Survey 2004/05.

The cost of caring for a disabled child is proportionately higher for a lone-parent family than for a two-parent family. This is not surprising, since in a two-parent family there are more parental resources to go round, so more help and assistance can be provided within the family. A lone parent is more likely to have to seek help outside the home – either travelling to a service provider or getting someone to come round, both of which are costly. Costs for both types of families are high. However, the results suggest that families with disabled children need incomes between 10% and 18% higher than similar families without disabled children, in order to secure the same standard of living.

Taking a family of average income (for the relevant family type) gives extra costs in the range of £62 to £74 per week (in 2004/05 prices; £68 to £82 in 2007 prices). This lies between the estimates from previous studies using alternative methods: the expenditure diaries approach produced a figure of £38 per week and the budget standards approach produced a figure of £119 per week. This is as we would expect. The budget standards approach reflects an aspiration – what parents think they *should* spend to create a level playing field for their child – which is likely to be higher than what they are actually able to spend. On the other hand, the expenditure diaries approach reflects only those costs that parents actually make and can directly attribute to the child. The standard of living approach lies in the middle. It reflects what parents actually spend, but takes into account, first, that spending might be reduced on adult consumption items in order to be able to meet the disabled child's needs and, second, that some general spending – heating the home, replacing broken furniture, transport, and so on – may be higher when there is a disabled child in the family, even though these are not specifically child-related categories of expenditure.

Table 2 compares poverty rates adjusted using the extra costs estimates in Table 1, with poverty rates calculated in the usual way (ie, with no adjustment for the extra costs of disabled children). Poverty rates using three different poverty lines – at 50%, 60% and 70% of median income for the whole population – are reported. The middle one, 60% of median income, is most often quoted in the UK, but the other thresholds give an indication of how sensitive the results are to using different poverty lines.

The table shows that adjustment for extra costs of disabled children makes little difference to overall poverty rates. This is because families with disabled children are a relatively small proportion of the overall population, and many of them are already counted among the poor, even before taking into account extra costs. Among individuals in lone-parent families, for example, the poverty rate (using the 60% of median income threshold) rises only slightly, from 31.3% to 32.2%, when the extra costs of disabled children are taken into account.[9]

However, if we focus on families with disabled children, the 'true' level of poverty, adjusting for extra costs, becomes clear. Table 3 compares families with

Table 2: Poverty rates with and without taking account of extra costs of disabled children

| | Unadjusted poverty rates | | | Poverty rates taking account of extra costs | | |
| | Below % of median | | | Below % of median | | |
	50	60	70	50	60	70
Lone-parent families	11.9	31.3	50.8	12.7	32.2	51.1
Two-parent families	6.3	11.8	19.8	6.3	11.9	20.0

Note: Income is before housing costs. Poverty lines calculated with reference to whole population.

Source: Family Resources Survey 2004/05.

Table 3: Poverty rates taking account of extra costs of disabled children, comparing families with and without disabled children

	Families without disabled children			Families with disabled children Unadjusted			Families with disabled children Taking account of extra costs		
	Below % of median			Below % of median			Below % of median		
	50	60	70	50	60	70	50	60	70
Lone-parent families	11.8	30.9	50.3	12.8	34.7	54.0	19.4	42.3	57.3
Two-parent families	6.2	11.5	19.3	7.2	14.4	24.7	7.9	15.8	27.0

Note: Income is before housing costs. Poverty lines calculated with reference to whole population.

Source: Family Resources Survey 2004/05.

and without disabled children. The left-hand column shows poverty rates for families without disabled children (which are the same whether or not one adjusts for extra costs), the middle column shows unadjusted poverty rates for families with disabled children, and the right-hand column shows poverty rates for families with disabled children, taking into account extra costs – in other words, our best estimate of the real rates of poverty for these families.

This shows that more than two in five individuals in lone-parent families with disabled children are in poverty (using 60% median income poverty threshold), compared with fewer than one in three individuals in lone-parent families without disabled children. For two-parent families with a disabled child, the adjusted poverty rate is about one in six, compared with one in nine for families without disabled children.

Conclusions

Money matters to families with disabled children because it enables them to offer their children the chance "to be normal and experience life" (Nicole, whose son has ADHD and is autistic).[10] In Nicole's case, a recent grant had enabled her to provide appropriate space in her home for her son to have friends round – essential, because his disability makes socialising outside the home difficult. Sometimes families cut back on other items to meet the direct costs of their child's disability. Getting a bit extra helps to restore spending on things which other families regard as normal: Jane, also interviewed for Preston's study, commented after being awarded DLA for her son, "now I can put things into their lunch boxes that the other kids have".[11]

Social security benefits such as DLA are a crucial contribution to levelling the playing field between children affected by disability and others. It fosters social inclusion for children at particularly high risk of disadvantage, because they face the 'double whammy' of impairment and low income. But as the results in this chapter show, the reach of DLA and other benefits is not sufficient to fully offset the extra costs experienced by families with disabled children, and these families remain at considerably greater risk of poverty.

The government's central child poverty targets are defined in terms of household income without taking any account of the extra costs of disability for children or adults. This means that even if the government were to meet its target, as currently defined, there would still be disabled children in poverty. The first step, then, is to acknowledge the scale and impact of extra costs on these families, and adjust the poverty statistics accordingly.

The second step is to do something about it – for example, extending eligibility for the relevant benefits and providing more goods and services for families with disabled children free of charge. The delivery strategy for the child poverty Public Service Agreement, shared by the Department for Work and Pensions and HM Treasury, includes measures to raise awareness and simplify the claims process for DLA.[12] This is certainly helpful, but it does not address the needs of families who are not entitled to benefits under current rules or who are entitled but do not receive enough to cover the extra costs they incur. Only if these unmet needs were addressed could the government claim to be on the way to fulfilling its aim, as stated in the recent disabled children review, of "ensuring that every disabled child can have the best possible start in life, and the support they and their families need to make equality of opportunity a reality, allowing each and every child to fulfil their potential".[13]

Notes

[1] Department for Work and Pensions, *Households Below Average Income 1994/95–2005/06*, 2007, Table 4.5, http://www.dwp.gov.uk/asd/hbai/hbai2006/contents.asp (accessed 9 November 2007).

[2] G Preston, *Helter Skelter: Families, disabled children and the benefit system*. CASE paper 92, Centre for Analysis of Social Exclusion, London School of Economics, 2005. http://sticerd.lse.ac.uk/dps/case/cp/CASEpaper92.pdf (accessed 9 November 2007).

[3] R Berthoud, J Lakey, and S McKay, *The Economic Problems of Disabled People*, Policy Studies Institute, London, 1993.

[4] A Zaidi and T Burchardt, 'Comparing incomes when needs differ: equivalisation for the extra costs of disability in the UK', *Review of Income and Wealth*, 51:1 (2005), pp. 89–114.

[5] B Dobson and S Middleton, *Paying to Care: The cost of childhood disability*, Joseph Rowntree Foundation, York, 1998.

[6] See N Smith, S Middleton, K Ashton-Brooks, L Cox and B Dobson with L Reigh, *Disabled People's Costs of Living: 'More than you would think'*, Joseph Rowntree Foundation, York, 2004. Smith and colleagues used a similar approach to calculate the extra costs of disabled adults.

[7] B Dobson, S Middleton and A Beardsworth, *The Impact of Childhood Disability on Family Life*, Joseph Rowntree Foundation, York, 2001.

[8] The savings indicator was used in our previous work on adults. See Zaidi and Burchardt (note 4).

[9] In order to retain a clear focus on disabled children, these results do not take into account the extra costs of disability among adults.

[10] Quoted in Preston, p. 36 (see note 2).

[11] Preston, p. 43 (see note 2).

[12] HM Treasury, *PSA Delivery Agreement 9: Halve the number of children in poverty by 2010–11, on the way to eradicating child poverty by 2020*, The Stationery Office, London, 2007, p.13. http://www.hm-treasury.gov.uk/media/B/9/pbr_csr07_psa9.pdf (accessed 19 December 2007).

[13] HM Treasury and Department for Education and Skills, (2007) *Aiming High for Disabled Children: Better support for families*, The Stationery Office, London, 2007 p.3.

4 Poverty, food and nutrition

Elizabeth Dowler

This chapter examines the relationship between household income, deprivation and children's experience of food in the UK. It includes evidence from surveys of children's dietary patterns and intakes of nutrients, and briefly discusses the health consequences of these observations. But food is more than a 'bundle of nutrients'; what we eat says a great deal about who we are, how we like to live, and what we value. These aspects are true for children too, though there are fewer research studies that capture what British children think about food these days. There is a great deal of anxiety at present about what children and young people are eating, at home and at school. The School Food Trust in England, and the reports *Hungry for Success* in Scotland, *Food and Fitness* in Wales, and *Fit Futures* in Northern Ireland, address some of these concerns, while recognising the scale of the problem. Parents, academics and civil society have put pressure on governments to address TV and other advertising of 'unhealthy' food. There are calls for better food provision in nurseries. It is recognised that things are likely to be worse for poorer children, though many blame parents for not maintaining more care over what their children eat.

The evidence about children's diets

It has long been acknowledged that food patterns, nutrient intakes and physical outcomes of growth and attained body size vary by indicators of social and economic conditions. Those who are better off are more likely to eat healthier diets than those who are poorer, to grow better as infants and young children, and to be a healthier body size when adult. However, the size of differences between classes varies by country, and in the UK is probably less significant now than early in the last century.[1] Usually, dietary differences by socio-economic class are more marked in parents' intakes, especially mothers', than in their children's. As you might expect, parents protect their children's diets as much as they can from the effects of living with insufficient money (see

34

Chapter 13). Nevertheless, differences can be observed even in young children and babies, as well as in older teenagers.

The annual UK-wide survey of household food and expenditure, which provides information on foods eaten and nutrients consumed per head, showed during the 1990s that intakes of vitamins, minerals and dietary fibre were much lower in poorer households than those that were more affluent. In terms of what foods people ate, those in poorer households had lower intakes of vegetables and (especially) fruit, and higher intakes of white bread, processed meats and sugar.[2]

The government also regularly measures what individuals are eating through national sample surveys on diet and nutrition, which are done for different age groups every five years or so. The two UK-wide surveys that carried out detailed measurements specifically on younger and older children are now about ten and seven years-old respectively, but there is no reason to suppose that patterns they revealed have changed very much, as a more recent survey of low-income households shows. In these earlier surveys, poorer children – defined as being in a household in receipt of benefits or where the household head is unemployed – were much less likely to eat the foods recommended for a healthy life, such as fruits and vegetables and wholemeal products, and were more likely to eat foods with more starchy carbohydrate, sugar and salt than is good for their health and wellbeing. Other national surveys, which use 'food frequency' measures rather than weighed intakes and occupational social class rather than income, give a similar picture. For instance, children in Scotland living in households classified as semi-routine and routine (which is roughly comparable to 'semi-skilled and unskilled') were twice as likely to have eaten no fruit and vegetables during the survey period as those in managerial and professional households.[3] These surveys also show that most young people drink more fizzy drinks than water or even fruit juice or milk, and that poorer children are no exception.[4] Children's diets are even more likely to be essentially cheap and less healthy where food and other basic goods are more expensive, such as in Northern Ireland.[5]

A UK-wide survey specifically on low-income households' diet and nutrition was published in 2007 by the Food Standards Agency.[6] In general, the findings on children, rather depressingly, were similar to those from the earlier surveys that looked at all children, despite recent government measures to improve children's food such as '5-a-Day' and free school fruit and vegetables. In this latest survey, children were more likely than the adults (in the same low-income households) to have eaten sausages, fried chicken, burgers, kebabs, pies or chips – especially if they were older. Four out of five children ate crisps and snacks daily, more than three out of five drank fizzy drinks, and all were much more likely than children in the previous surveys to eat pizza and to drink whole milk. Very few children indeed ate any fish (recommended as part of a healthy diet); on average they ate fewer than two portions of fruit and vegetables a day (the recommendation is five daily portions), and this was particularly true of older children. If we look specifically at nutrients, all the national surveys show that here, too, the intake is likely to be at lower levels in young people of lower socio-economic status, because of the type of food they eat rather than the quantity (although some poor children do eat less food). Poorer children also tend to have lower blood or urine markers for folate, riboflavin, vitamins C and D, and iron.

The evidence about children's health outcome

One obvious health outcome of diet is growth patterns or body size. For many years it was recognised that children living in low-income households were more likely to be short and thin for their age. Increasingly nowadays, children in low-income households are more likely to be overweight or obese. They do not obtain the right balance of micronutrients from their diet because, as the surveys have shown, they eat disproportionate amounts of refined sugar, salt and saturated fats and too few fruits and vegetables, unprocessed meat, wholemeal cereals and oily fish. In the recent Food Standards Agency survey, more than one-third of those in the younger age groups were overweight, and one-fifth were already obese; very few were found to be underweight.[7] The prevalence of overweight was nearly twice as high in girls living with a lone parent than in those living with two or more adults. The same survey showed that half of the younger children and one-third of older children report very low levels of physical activity (less than 30 minutes a day). A great deal is being said about overweight and obesity in children at present, but rates are probably increasing faster among poorer children.[8] It has been known for some time that poorer women are more likely to be overweight or obese than richer women; now this distinction is being seen in children and young people, and to some extent in men too. Recent research suggests that the likelihood of childhood obesity can be predicted by both household income and the wider social and economic environment in which children live.[9, 10] This is not surprising. Body size is an outcome of both dietary intake and energy expenditure (which is why the dual findings of the Food Standards Agency survey are so serious), as well as early life experience, and these depend not only on an individual's decisions about food and physical activity, which link to family and friends' norms of behaviour, but on the opportunities and possibilities in children's social and physical environment. Children who live in run-down estates or in dilapidated private rental houses are less likely to go outside to play, or belong to clubs, and are more likely to live where cheap fast-food is easily available. There is considerable social and psychological stigma to being obese, especially for children, which works against being active and enjoying sport, and this has implications for future health.

These poor household circumstances and deprived neighbourhoods may be building on the biology of early life experiences. Poor children in the UK are still more likely than richer children to be born smaller. Preterm birth (earlier than 37 weeks' gestation) and low birthweight, both of which are more prevalent among poorer mothers, are closely associated with infant death and, for those who survive, chronic diseases in later life.[11] Poorer/lower social class mothers are less likely to initiate or maintain breastfeeding,[12] a practice which is important for the health of mothers and children, both immediately and over a lifetime. For example, babies who are not breastfed are many times more likely to get infections such as gastroenteritis in their first year, and may be more susceptible to allergies and conditions like eczema. Babies who are not breastfed, or who are given standard infant formula, have lower IQ (including verbal IQ) detectable even aged eight, and those who are not breastfed may be more likely to become obese in later childhood or young adulthood – and this type of obesity is harder to treat.[13]

Nutrition in early life probably also has a big impact on brain development; at certain critical periods, diet seems to be crucial for health and performance later on. Dietary deficiencies and poor nutritional status in children, even in milder forms (especially iron-deficiency anaemia), probably have detrimental effects on cognitive development, behaviour, concentration and school performance. Measurement and attribution of these effects, separating out that of subsequent environments, is difficult, but children who go to school hungry or tired, or generally poorly nourished, cannot learn properly or benefit from teaching, because they show impaired memory and attention span, and reduced efficiency of learning (information processing). They are more likely to truant or leave school early.

The longer-term health impacts are also very serious: the kind of diet poorer children mostly eat, combined with low levels of physical activity, is likely to lead to higher rates of coronary heart disease, high blood pressure, stroke and various cancers. It is also linked to non-insulin dependent diabetes, which is now increasingly observed among children (it used to be known as 'adult-onset').[14] These dietary factors, combined with the greater likelihood of smoking in poorer households, contribute to the widely recognised differentials in adult mortality. Those who live in the most affluent electoral wards can expect to live, on average, 10 to 15 years longer than those living in the poorest, and the origins of this difference go right back to childhood and even infancy.[15]

Why do these differences persist?

Are we simply measuring the effect of people's ignorance about what is healthy and good to eat, or their attitude of not caring much and preferring to eat 'what they like'? It probably isn't that simple. The major trends shaping contemporary food consumption, including the increasing availability and promotion of highly processed and ready-prepared foods and meals, and the intense growth of food marketing, particularly to children and young people, have been compounded until recently by the government's failure to pay sufficient attention to food in relation to social policy, school meal services and standards, and welfare.[16]

In the surveys referred to above, the differentials seen are more marked when intakes and food patterns are compared by household income, economic activity (employed versus unemployed/receiving state benefits) or household composition, than by occupation or parental education level, which are to some extent proxy indicators of wealth, cultural and social capital.[17] In other words, markers of poverty and deprivation show up worse diets more clearly than do markers of class or cultural differences.

The majority of people, whatever their social class and cultural or ethnic identity, buy their food from the four major retailers (Tesco, Sainsbury's, Asda and Morrison). These shops increasingly sell cook-chill 'ready-made' meals or quick-to-assemble ingredients (for instance, dried pasta and instant sauces). Whether or not poorer people buy more 'ready meals' than richer people do, they are more likely to choose the familiar kinds. They may also rely on fast foods more often than do richer households – because they are 'filling', quite cheap and readily available. For those with little money the main factors governing purchase are usually cost and familiarity – knowing that family members will eat and be satisfied by what is bought. There is little scope for trying out new things. And although many low-income families are out of work, or only work part-time because they have caring responsibilities, low-income families can also be in full-time work,[18] often working long and unsociable hours. For them, reliance on 'ready meals' and 'fast foods' may be difficult to avoid when parents are tired and need to feed a family quickly.

Much has been made of the loss of cooking skills; this may be particularly the case for younger parents in general. Public and state concern is often focused on lower socio-economic groups, although the evidence that poorer households' skills are worse is equivocal.[19] At any rate there is much anecdotal evidence of a desire for skills improvement. Many younger, poorer mothers are clearly empowered by 'cook and eat' as well as 'healthy eating' sessions provided by volunteers or health workers, which give them confidence in their own capacity to feed their children well.[20]

The rise in obesity and its potential costs to society have sharpened the ongoing debate in the UK on the damaging effect of TV and other advertising on food purchasing, particularly that geared to children, which it is argued is more likely to promote highly processed and unhealthy food.[21] The evidence is mixed about whether poorer children watch more commercial television, or whether they live where there are more likely to be fast-food shops.[22] Findings do suggest that children whose families are poorer are more likely to be eating the foods heavily promoted by advertisements. There is probably a mixture of reasons for this: poorer mothers often do not have enough money to buy 'healthier' foods on a regular basis; there may be fewer shops selling them near where they live; and those who left school with fewer qualifications and are young themselves are less likely to be confident enough to resist the advertisers' messages.

Children's experience of food in nurseries and school is a very important one, not only in determining what they eat, but in shaping their thinking and learning about what good food tastes like, and the pleasures of eating with peers. Children and young people are quite independent contemporary consumers: if institutions do not provide what they think they want, they increasingly go elsewhere (to the local chip shop, for instance). Schools that have worked to improve understanding about how food is grown and prepared, involving children of different ages in selecting menus and even in preparing food, or running tuck shops, find it less difficult to persuade reluctant customers to purchase and eat 'healthier' menus, and this is true of poorer children as well as richer. However, the quality of food provided free for those eligible to claim (a smaller number than those who live in low-income households) is obviously very important – and variable around the country.[23]

Poorer households spend a much higher proportion of income on food than the richest households (about twice as high), although the actual amount they spend is considerably lower – only about £35 a week in the poorest lone-parent families.[24] What you can buy for that money of course depends on which shops you can get to, what is available and how much you have to pay. Large supermarkets, which are not always easily accessible to those on low incomes, can usually sell foods at lower prices than small corner shops because of their greater buying power and much larger economies of scale.[25] They can also afford to discount basic goods such as bread and milk as 'loss leaders'. If families have to add bus or taxi fares to their food bill, there is less money available for 'luxuries' such as fruit or low-salt/low-fat versions of familiar foods.

Furthermore, costs of rent, fuel, council tax and other basics have increased faster in recent years than benefits or, in many cases, wages. Food is usually where people have to cut back to meet these pressing demands on their purse. State benefits have consistently been shown insufficient to enable people to purchase the food needed for good health, even at mainstream supermarket prices, and certainly not if they have to rely on local stores. Research which looked at what a single person working full-time could buy if paid at the hourly minimum wage rate found that this, too, was insufficient to cover the costs of goods and rent to meet healthy living guidelines.[26]

Conclusions

Families living on the lowest incomes usually do manage to feed themselves through careful budgeting and ingenuity, but what they can afford to eat is monotonous and unlikely to consistently meet healthy eating guidelines. They are less likely to have friends round for meals or parties; they miss out on entertaining, reciprocity and the social aspects of food that are central to our society. Birthdays, Christmas and other festivals become occasions for dread instead of celebrations and affirmation. Children learn that food is flexible: it is where you cut back, and is only for 'filling up'. Shopping and eating become stressful and miserable, instead of the opportunities for pleasure they represent where money is not tight. The consequences for health and wellbeing of scrimping and not eating well because of lack of money are extremely serious.

This chapter draws on material in E Dowler, M Caraher and P Lincoln, 'Inequalities in food and nutrition: challenging "lifestyles"', in E Dowler and N Spencer (eds) *Challenging Health Inequalities: From Acheson to 'Choosing Health'*, Bristol, Policy Press, 2007.

Notes

[1] E Dowler, M Caraher and P Lincoln, 'Inequalities in food and nutrition: challenging lifestyles', in E Dowler and N Spencer (eds) *Challenging Health Inequalities: From Acheson to 'Choosing Health'*, Policy Press, Bristol, 2007, pp. 127–55.

[2] E Dowler and S Turner with B Dobson, *Poverty Bites: Good, health and poor families*, Child Poverty Action Group, London, 2001.

[3] C Bromley, K Sproston and N Shelton (eds) *The Scottish Health Survey 2003*, Volume 3: Children, Healthier Scotland, The Scottish Executive, Edinburgh, 2005. http://www.scotland.gov.uk/Resource/Doc/76169/0019732.pdf

[4] K Sproston and P Primatesta (eds) *Health Survey for England 2002*, The Stationery Office, London, 2003. http://www.archive2.official-documents.co.uk/document/deps/doh/survey02/hcyp/hcyp01.htm

[5] http://www.childrenslawcentre.org/ParticularCircumstancesofChildreninNorthernIreland-GorettiHorgan.htm (accessed 10 January 2007).

[6] M Nelson, B Ehrens, B Bates, S Church and T Boshier, *Low Income Diet and Nutrition Survey*, vols 1, 2 and 3, The Stationery Office, London, 2007. http://www.food.gov.uk/science/dietarysurveys/lidnsbranch/#h_5

[7] Nelson *et al*, vol. 3 (see note 6).

[8] J Armstrong, A R Dorosty, J J Reilly et al, 'Coexistence of social inequalities in undernutrition and obesity in pre-school children', *Archives of Disease in Childhood*, 88 (2003), pp. 671–75; House of Commons Health Committee, *Obesity*, third report of Session 2003/04, 1: HC 23–1, The Stationery Office, London, 2004.

[9] E Stamatakis, P Primatesta, S Chinn, R Rona and E Flascheti, 'Overweight and obesity trends from 1974–2003 in English children: what is the role of socioeconomic factors?', *Archives of the Diseases of Childhood*, 90 (2005), pp. 999–1004.

[10] S Kinra, R P Nelder and G J Lewendon, 'Deprivation and childhood obesity: a cross sectional study of 20,973 children in Plymouth, United Kingdom', *Journal of Epidemiology and Community Health*, 54 (2000), pp. 456–60; S Kinra, J H Baumer and G Davey Smith, 'Early growth and childhood obesity: a historical cohort study', *Archives of Disease in Childhood*, 90 (2005), pp. 1122–27.

[11] N Spencer, C Law, 'Inequalities in pregnancy and early years and the impact across the life course: progress and future challenges', in E Dowler and N Spencer (eds) *Challenging Health Inequalities: From Acheson to Choosing Health*, Policy Press, Bristol, 2007, pp. 69–93.

[12] N Beale, G Kane, M Gwynne, C Peart, G Taylor, D Herrick, A Boyd, and ALSPAC Study Team, Council tax valuation band predicts breast feeding and socio-economic status in the ALSPAC study population, 2006 accessed online (10.11.07) new reference inserted http://www.biomedcentral.com/1471-2458/6/5

[13] L Li, T J Parsons, C Power, 'Breast feeding and obesity in childhood: cross sectional study', *British Medical Journal*, 327 (2003), pp. 904–05; K B Michels, W C Willett, B I Graubard *et al*, 'A longitudinal study of infant feeding and obesity throughout life course', *International Journal of Obesity*, 31 (2007), pp. 1078–85. This effect of breast feeding is independent of subsequent living conditions and socio-economic status.

[14] Dowler *et al* (see note 1); World Cancer Research Fund/American Institute for Cancer Research, *Food, Nutrition, Physical Activity, and the Prevention of Cancer: A Global Perspective*, AICR, Washington, DC, 2007.

[15] Department of Health, *Choosing Health: making healthier choices easier*, Department of Health, London, 2004, p. 83.

[16] T Lang and M Heasman, *Food Wars*, Earthscan, London, 2004; M Nestle, *Food Politics: How the food industry influences nutrition and health*, University of California Press, Berkeley, Calif., 2002.

[17] Department of Food, Environment and Rural Affairs, *Family Food: Report on the Expenditure & Food Survey*, DEFRA, London, 2006; W L Wrieden, K L Barton, J Armstrong and G McNeill, *A Review of Food Consumption and Nutrient Intakes from National Surveys in Scotland: Comparison to the Scottish Dietary Targets*, Food Standards Agency Scotland, Aberdeen, 2006.

[18] G Palmer, T MacInnes and P Kenway, *Monitoring poverty and social exclusion 2007*, Joseph Rowntree Foundation, York, 2007.

[19] M Caraher, T Lang, P Dixon. and R Carr-Hill, R. (1999) 'The state of cooking in England: The relationship of cooking skills to food choice', *British Food Journal*, 101:8 (1999), pp. 590–609.

[20] For example, http://www.foodvision.gov.uk/pages/cooking-skills; Community Food and Health (Scotland), *A taste for independence: Using food to develop skills for life*, Scottish Consumer Council, Glasgow, 2007. (http://www.communityfoodandhealth.org.uk/fileuploads/cfhstasteforindependence-8048.pdf)

[21] http://www.ofcom.org.uk/media/mofaq/bdc/foodadsfaq/; G Hastings, M Stead *et al*, *Review of Research on the Effects of Food Promotion to Children*, report prepared for the Food Standards Agency, Glasgow: Centre for Social Marketing, 2003; M Caraher, J Landon and K Dalmeny, 'Television advertising and children: lessons from policy development', *Public Health Nutrition*, 9:5 (2006), pp. 596–605.

[22] S Cummins and S Macintyre, 'Food environments and obesity – neighbourhood or nation?', *International Journal of Epidemiology*, 35 (2005), pp. 100–04; A M Prentice and S A Jebb, 'Fast foods, energy density and obesity: a possible mechanistic link', *Obesity Reviews*, 4 (2003), pp 187–94; R Sturm and A Datar, 'Body Mass Index in Elementary School Children, Metropolitan Area Food Prices and Food Outlet Density', *Public Health*, 119 (2005), pp. 1059–68.

[23] M Nelson, K Lowes, V Hwang and members of the Nutrition Group, School Meals Review Panel, DfES, 'The contribution of school meals to food consumption and nutrient intakes of young people aged 4–18 years in England', *Public Health Nutrition*, 10:7, pp. 652–62.

[24] On average in 2005/06, households spent £45.30, or 10% of their expenditure, a week on food and non-alcoholic drinks. The poorest 10% of households spent only £33 a week (15% of expenditure), compared with nearly £60 a week (7% of expenditure) in the richest 10% of households (using equivalised income deciles). http://www.statistics.gov.uk/downloads/theme_social/Family_Spending_2005-06/Familyspending2005-06.pdf (accessed 10 November 2007).

[25] For instance: M White, J Bunting, E Williams, S Raybould, A Adamson and JC Mathers, *Do 'Food Deserts' Exist?: A multi-level, geographical analysis of the relationship between retail food access, socio-economic position and dietary intake*, Food Standards Agency, London, 2004.

[26] J Morris, A Donkin, D Wonderling, P Wilkinson and E Dowler, 'A minimum income for healthy living', *Journal of Epidemiology and Community Health*, 54 (2000), pp. 885–89; http://www.z2k.org/The-pain-of-poverty-in-the-UK-June-2006.doc (accessed 10 November 2007).

5 Lone parents and the challenge to make work pay

Lesley Hoggart and Sandra Vegeris

Introduction

Tackling child poverty through parental employment remains high on the government's agenda. This is a central theme of the recent Department for Work and Pension's (DWP's) document, *Ready for work: full employment in our generation,*[1] and it is underscored by the recently created Child Poverty Unit. One key target group for this policy agenda has remained constant: lone parents, 95% of whom are women.[2]

There are currently more than one million lone parents in work, constituting a significant proportion (57%) of all lone-parent families. An employment rise of 11 percentage points over the past ten years has been attributed to favourable economic conditions and government initiatives such as the voluntary New Deal for Lone Parents, and more aggressive measures such as the mandatory Work Focused Interviews. But the date for the government's target of achieving 70% employment among lone parents – 2010 – is rapidly approaching. This explains the hard-nosed proposals set out by DWP. Lone parents are among the 250,000 non-working individuals being targeted with radical and ambitious policies that expect people to engage more actively in the labour market. Most contentious are the government's intentions to impose further requirements on lone parents to seek work (or face benefit sanctions if they do not do so) when their youngest child is 12 (2008), and when their youngest child is 7 (2010).

Lone parents who make the transition from benefits, however, generally end up on relatively low earnings, often part-time hours supplemented by working tax credits. Recent data from the Families and Children Study (FACS) reveal that the average weekly income of a working lone-parent family in 2005 was £318 and one-third of this consisted of benefits and tax credits.[3] This represents 70% of the average (equivalised) income of a single-earner couple family in which one-fifth of the income is typically subsidised by the State. This shortfall is partly accounted for by the high proportion of lone-parent earners who work part-time hours (16 to 29 hours), at nearly 50% among those working.[4]

This chapter raises some critical questions for policy. Drawing on recent research, it focuses on the work experiences of lone parents, most of whom had recently entered low-paid, part-time employment. The chapter first looks at the struggle to be 'better off' in work. It then looks at the difficulties that part-time working lone parents face when they attempt to improve their earnings position.

Working lives

When lone parents enter work, many are likely to find themselves in low-paid, low-skilled, unstable part-time employment. This has been shown in a number of studies. The British Lone Parent Cohort, for example, tracked a representative sample of 988 lone parents between 1991 and 2001. At the start, only 27% were in paid work of 16 or more hours. This rose to 56% over the ten years, while a further 17% had left work they had taken up over the period.[5] Further analysis of the same data set, however, revealed that, of the 560 lone parents who participated in the full study, nearly half of those who entered work experienced significant work instability.[6] Over the decade most of the steady workers remained in low-paid jobs[7] and more than one-third who were not low paid at the start were low paid at the end of the observation period. This was in part attributed to the low-skilled work most of these lone parents entered into.

Other research that has tracked lone parents over time has identified work sustainability as a difficult issue.[8] Lone parents included in the working statistics at any one time are not, therefore, necessarily remaining in work. One study has shown that a substantial proportion (up to 20%) of those who left benefits to go into work had returned to benefits within ten months,[9] while another suggests that lone parents were almost twice as likely to leave their job as non-lone parents, and one-third more likely than single childless women.[10] There was also a clear connection with low pay: one-third of those who worked over the period 1999 to 2003 were persistently low paid (with a further 40% being low paid over part of the period), and low-paid lone parents were twice as likely to leave work than those who were not low paid.[11]

Research also suggests that even when a lone-parent family appears to be financially better off in work, extra expenses can rapidly build up and challenge their financial stability. Prior to work entry, Jobcentre Plus can perform a 'better-off calculation' to compare income on benefits with potential employment-generated income. This calculation, designed to provide hard data to help lone parents decide about the financial feasibility of work, is increasingly becoming routine during a Work Focused Interview. But the calculation has been criticised for providing a too simplistic representation of the real costs associated with work.[12] Extra expenses can include work clothing, travel expenses, childcare, school dinners, school trips and school uniform. In addition, it does not take into account debt repayments that are held in check until work begins.

The stresses associated with struggling to make ends meet are complicated by other strains of a working lone-parent family. Qualitative research has shed light on how unstable and difficult life can be for lone-parent families experiencing their first years in paid work.[13, 14, 15] In their study following 50 lone parents and their children, Jane Millar and Tess Ridge found that half had already changed the nature of their jobs within the first year of work, while some had experienced changes in their personal circumstances.[16] Nearly half of the families did not perceive themselves to be better off compared with when they were not working and receiving income support. Crucially, this assessment incorporated views on future income security, as some of these parents were on volatile earnings. Unstable contract positions, debt repayments and costs not previously incurred, such as transport, childcare, school uniform and meals, all needed to be taken into the balance.

Indeed, when the household dynamics of budgeting on low work earnings are combined with the less savoury aspects of low-skilled, part-time work, it becomes clearer why job retention can be a difficult issue for lone parents. Much part-time work is characterised by limited opportunities and poor employment conditions.[17] Some of this work is tied to a fixed-term contract, it often does not include sick pay or holiday pay, and it can require working unsociable hours. Other threats to job retention centre on dissatisfaction with the work itself and inflexible employers, particularly in relation to childcare needs.[18] The complex arrangements lone parents endure to combine employment and care responsibilities have been well documented.[19]

It is most often a combination of these factors (job and family-related) that lead to a lone parent coming out of work. But it is also evident that being financially better off in work does not necessarily compensate for the other difficulties faced by working lone parents. This chapter next discusses how these difficulties can present themselves some time after lone parents have settled in work, and how difficult it is for them to improve their situations.

Ongoing challenges

This section focuses on two recent qualitative studies documenting lone parents' experiences during their first years in work. Both studies were evaluations of labour market interventions that offered various supports to lone parents who had recently entered work. The In-Work Credit (IWC) pilot provided an earnings supplement of £40 per week for up to 52 weeks. The Employment Retention and Advancement (ERA) intervention offered ongoing advisory support, financial help for emergencies and payments for training, as well as an in-work payment of £400 every four months (for those working 30 or more hours per week).[20] All of the lone parents were on low earnings that qualified them for working tax credits.

Echoing other studies, these lone parents talked about the first few months in work being very difficult financially, and, in particular, about being 'bombarded' with demands to pay bills, or pay back debts. They then contrasted their financial situation when settled in work to their situation before entering work. Although, in general, they assessed their financial status more favourably in work, this was often only because of extra supports (such as tax credits) that had been put in place, plus the financial bonuses. These supports often made it possible for them to move into poorly paid jobs, and the extra money was generally used for day-to-day living expenses (utility bills, food and transport). It was also clear that for some the extra cash did make a real difference between severe financial hardship and just managing. In these cases, there was likely to be a new struggle when the extra payments came to an end:

> *"And when the Jobcentre stopped that in-work credit, that crippled me, because that were £40 a week. And even though they said at the beginning, 'This is only*

for one year', when it stopped – I mean it was £160 a month, it was a lot of money – I'm still suffering from that."

Only when given the opportunity to follow lone parents in work over an extended time period does it become clear that significant difficulties can occur at any point beyond the first weeks and months in work, and that change is constant. One participant in the ERA study felt that she needed to work through a full year of annual events in her family life before she could establish a rhythm. For her, important events included expenditure related to: the September school start, Christmas, children's birthdays, a family holiday and covering childcare on school holidays. It was also evident from other working lone parents' experiences that low-paid work provided an insufficient buffer against unexpected expenditure like an extra bill or when time off work for illness meant reduced income.

The time frame of the studies also helped provide valuable insights into the ongoing struggles of working lone parents to improve their financial situations. The main options considered were: moving to full-time work; trying to find 'better' part-time work; or improving skills through training.

ERA offered an interesting challenge to lone parents: if they worked 30 or more hours they would be rewarded with extra income. Although some did increase their hours, many chose not to despite this incentive. For those who increased work hours, two factors were important: their employer was amenable to offering more hours; and they felt that the 'time was right' for them and their families. Their decision centred on what they felt was best for their children, and many thought that full-time work was not compatible with their vision of 'good parenting'. One lone parent explained why her attempt to work full time had failed:

"I wasn't there for the children, I wasn't doing much, I was always just too tired. So I gave that up and I had a break for a couple of months, and now I've gone back to work 16 hours."

In our research, the majority of lone parents preferred to work within school hours in such a way that their children would not notice their absence, or they wanted to work school term times to guarantee they would have school holidays with their children (and eliminate the need for childcare). For younger families, the desire to avoid the need for childcare was the biggest driver for part-time employment. Working part-time therefore served as a compromise position in the labour market. Part-time work, however, tended to be poorly paid, with limited opportunities for better-paid work offered by employers.

ERA participants talked about the difficulties of finding alternative 'better' work. One lone parent felt significantly worse off in work because she was never paid when she, or her son, was ill. She desperately wanted a similar job with improved pay and working conditions but, during the two years on the programme, no suitable options became available:

> *"I want more admin work, but I want to get into something, either Civil Service or Council, somewhere where you've got your rights – sick pay and things like that – which I don't get in the job that I'm in. But obviously at the moment I can't see anything like that around and I'm also tied with a young child and I've got to fit everything around him."*

Another option for lone parents was combining training with work, often as a longer-term strategy towards finding a better paid job in the future. The ERA programme offered financial support for such training. Some lone parents were willing to set aside more immediate financial gain in order to invest time in developing new skills. Once again, however, this was far from an 'easy option'.

Many were not able to take up the opportunities because their employers were not amenable to adjusting work schedules around training courses. Others felt that they wanted to do the training, but they could not fit it in. This meant additional hours away from the family, either attending a course or doing home study. Similarly, courses were often only offered in the evenings, which would require the use of childcare, or during hours that were not compatible with their work.

Another time-related issue was the parent's immediate circumstances and what they thought was right for their family. Some perceived the prospect of training positively but felt this was something for the future.[21] This sentiment was most common among mothers with greater caring responsibilities (eg, younger children, larger families) and among those with little previous work experience. Staff who delivered the ERA programme reported that it was not uncommon for a lone parent to warm to the idea of training once they had settled into a work routine. But the time frame for this relied a great deal on individual and family circumstances.

Conclusions

Working part-time hours, and sustaining work at this rate, is often the most feasible option for lone parents. They are prepared to make financial sacrifices in order to devote time to ensure their children are properly cared for.

However, part-time work holds income down. Many lone parents struggle to manage a job and a family, in part exacerbated by a low income. As government policy continues to focus on increasing the numbers of lone parents in work and in keeping them there, more resources need to be channelled into programmes and initiatives that improve the prospects for part-time workers. Among these strategies ought to be measures that make part-time work more affordable.

Notes

[1] Department for Work and Pensions (DWP), *Ready for Work: Full employment in our generation*, report presented to Parliament by the Secretary of State for Work and Pensions, December 2007: http://www.dwp.gov.uk/welfarereform/readyforwork/readyforwork.pdf

[2] L Hoxhallari, A Conolly and N Lyon, *Families with Children in Britain: Findings from the 2005 Families and Children Study (FACS)*, DWP Research Report no. 424, Corporate Document Services (CDS), Leeds, 2007.

[3] L Hoxhallari, A Conolly and N Lyon, *Families with Children in Britain: Findings from the 2005 Families and Children Study (FACS)*, DWP Research Report no. 424, Corporate Document Services (CDS), Leeds, 2007.

[4] In 1997 the Organisation for Economic Co-operation and Development (OECD) set 30 hours as the cut-off point to delineate part-time and full-time work. Here, the lower parameter is tied to working tax credit eligibility rules, which set the threshold at a minimum of 16 hours.

[5] A Marsh and S Vegeris, *The British Lone Parent Cohort and their Children: 1991 to 2001*, DWP Research Report no. 209, CDS, Leeds, 2004.

[6] K Stewart, K, *Employment Trajectories for Mothers in Low-skilled Work: Evidence from the British Lone Parent Cohort*, Centre for Analysis of Social Exclusion Casepaper 122, London School of Economics, London, 2007.

[7] Low pay was defined as two-thirds of the male median wage.

[8] See A Yeo, *Experience of Work and Job Retention among Lone Parents: An evidence review*, DWP Working Paper no. 37, 2006; and also S Harkness (2006) 'Lone parents cycling in and out of benefits', in K Bell *et al*, *Staying On, Stepping Up: How can employment retention and advancement policies be made to work for lone parents?*, One Parent Families, London, 2006.

[9] J Hales, W Roth, M Barnes, J Millar, C Lessof, M Gloyer and A Shaw, *Evaluation of the New Deal for Lone Parents: Early lessons from the phase one prototype – findings of surveys*, Department of Social Security Research Report no. 109, CDS, Leeds, 2000.

[10] M Evans, S Harkness and R Arigoni Ortiz, (2004) *Lone Parents Cycling between Work and Benefits*, DWP Research Report, WAE217, CDS, Leeds, 2004.

[11] See Evans *et al*, note 9.

[12] SPAN, *Proofed for Parents by Parents: Participatory one parent proofing – Findings*, Single Parent Action Network, Bristol, 2007.

[13] J Millar, 'Better-off in work? Work, security and welfare for lone mothers', in C Glendinning and P Kemp (eds) *Cash and Care*, The Policy Press, Bristol, 2006.

[14] T Ridge, 'Helping out at home: Children's contributions to sustaining work and care in lone-mother families', in Glendinning and Kemp (see note 12).

[15] T Ridge, 'It's a family affair: Low-income children's perspectives on maternal work', *Journal of Social Policy*, 36:3 (2007), pp. 399–416.

[16] J Millar, 'The dynamics of poverty and employment: The contribution of qualitative longitudinal research to understanding transitions, adaptations and trajectories', *Social Policy & Society*, 6:4 (2007), pp. 533–44.

[17] J Millar, T Ridge and F Bennett, *Part-time Work and Social Security: Increasing the options?*, DWP Research Report no. 351, CDS, Leeds, 2006.

[18] L Hoggart, V Campbell-Barr, K Ray and S Vegeris, *Staying in Work and Moving Up: Evidence from the UK Employment Retention and Advancement (ERA) demonstration*, DWP Research Report no. 381, CDS, Leeds, 2006.

[19] See, for example, A Bell, N Finch, I La Valle, R Sainsbury and C Skinner, *A Question of Balance: Lone parents, childcare and work*, DWP Research Report no. 230, CDS, Leeds, 2005.

[20] For details on IWC refer to: K Ray, S Vegeris, S Brooks, V Campbell-Barr, L Hoggart, K Mackinnon and I Shutes, *The Lone Parents Pilots: A qualitative evaluation of Quarterly Work Focused Interviews (12+), Work Search Premium and In Work Credit*, DWP Research Report no. 423, CDS, Leeds, 2007. For details on ERA refer to: R Dorset, V Campbell-Barr, G Hamilton, L Hoggart, A Marsh, C Miller, J Phillips, K Ray, J Riccio, S Rich and S Vegeris, *Implementation and First-year Impacts of the UK Employment Retention Advancement (ERA) demonstration*, DWP Research Report no. 412, CDS: Leeds, 2007.

[21] Refer to Chapter 5 in Hoggart *et al* (see note 17).

6 Debt and savings

Karen Rowlingson and Stephen McKay

Background

Most people are able to keep up with their credit commitments and pay their bills on time without too much difficulty, but nearly 3 million people (in 2 million households) in 2005 said it was a constant struggle to do so. About half this number, 1.5 million people, said they were falling behind with payments, and about half a million said they had real financial problems.[1]

Ruth Lister has argued that people experiencing poverty live in a "vulnerability context", which makes it very difficult to cope with income shocks, despite their best efforts to make ends meet.[2] She concedes that savings could play an important part in strengthening people's capacity to deal with unexpected demands on, or drops in, income. However, she points out that there may be dangers in encouraging people on very low incomes to save if this means sacrificing their immediate living standards.

This chapter considers the extent of financial difficulties in relation to both problem debt and difficulties in saving. It also considers the causes and consequences of financial difficulties and whether or not the problem is due to the attitudes and low levels of financial capability among those on low income.

The extent of debt problems, financial difficulties and lack of savings

Debt problems are concentrated among particular groups of the population – especially those on low incomes, families with children and young people. Research has found that 42% of those in poverty were seriously behind with repaying bills or credit commitments in the previous year (compared with 4% among the non-poor).[3] Families with children, especially lone parents, have particularly high rates of poverty and debt.

Using the Families and Children Study (FACS), a study published in 2004 identified three groups: those 'never', 'sometimes' and 'always' in arrears.[4] Lone parents and Income Support recipients were the most likely to be 'always' in arrears.

The study also found relatively frequent movement in and out of arrears: one-third of families with arrears cleared them within a year while a quarter of those with no arrears accumulated them. Arrears in household bills were more persistent than arrears in credit commitments or housing costs.

The link between debt problems, age and low income is an interesting one. A survey of 'over-indebtedness' in 2002[5] found that four in ten of householders in their twenties had been in arrears in the previous 12 months and 37% currently either were in arrears or said they were in financial difficulty. The level of difficulties then declined steeply with age, and this is partly due to higher incomes among older people. But this link between age, income and financial problems does not quite work with pensioners as they have relatively low incomes and yet tend to avoid debt despite low incomes.[6, 7]

It is worth noting that those on the very lowest incomes do not have the very greatest debt problems. For example, the 2002 over-indebtedness survey found that it was households with gross incomes of between £5,000 and £7,500 that faced greater debt problems than those on even lower incomes. This may be because the slightly higher income group contains a large proportion of lone parents, while the lowest income group is mostly single people.[8] In other words it may not be household income *per se* that is linked to the risk of financial difficulties, but income in relation to family composition. Also, people on very low incomes tend to avoid taking on credit commitments, while those on high incomes take on commitments but can typically manage to repay them. It is those towards the lower-middle of the income distribution who therefore tend to have the greatest debt problems, not least when credit that was once affordable becomes more difficult to repay because of job loss or a drop in income.[9]

People on low incomes, not surprisingly, find it very difficult to save.[10] A study published in 2002 found that three in five people in households with net weekly incomes of below £150 had no formal savings, compared with only one in three of the population as a whole.[11] The Poverty and Social Exclusion

Survey, published in 2006, specifically asked whether people could afford to make regular savings of at least £10 per month 'for a rainy day' or towards retirement. Three-quarters of those classified as 'poor', compared with 7% of the 'non-poor', said that they were unable to do so.[12]

Employment and life-stage factors are also linked to saving behaviour: unemployed and disabled people, young single people, young couples with children, lone parents and those who have experienced major life changes such as divorce are all less likely to have savings. Many of those on a low income simply cannot afford to put money into formal saving accounts 'for a rainy day'.

Causes and consequences of financial problems

This chapter has highlighted the links between debt problems, savings and other factors (such as poverty, unemployment, family composition, age, etc.), but these links are quite complex. For example, it is clearly very difficult for people who experience persistent poverty and low income to avoid debt and to build savings. In this respect, poverty causes financial problems. But financial problems can also lead to poverty. The complex links between causes and consequences can perhaps be best illustrated in relation to separation and divorce. Financial problems can put a strain on couples, leading to (or contributing to) separation and divorce. In turn, separation and divorce can cause (further) financial problems and this is particularly clear from the extent of financial problems suffered by lone parents.

Another cause (and possible consequence) of financial problems is job loss. For example, secondary analysis of the British Household Panel Survey (BHPS) for 1991–2000 found that unemployment was the life event most associated with ceasing to save.[13] Reduction in income was also important, with a drop in earnings of 10% or more causing four out of ten of those who had been saving to stop. There is also a strong link between debt and changes in income. For example, a quarter of households that had experienced a drop in income in the previous 12 months were currently in arrears with one or more commitments, and a further two in ten said they were experiencing financial difficulties.[14] Earlier research had shown that loss of income through unemployment can have a sustained effect on the household budget, with an increased level of arrears up to three years later.[15]

Some qualitative research has suggested that job loss can cause debt and also that arrears can form a barrier to paid work. However, it has been found that arrears do not reduce movements into work among lone parents.[16] And among couples, those with arrears were actually slightly more likely to move into employment than those without. There was evidence, however, that among workers, arrears led to leaving employment (possibly because of problems with housing benefit and tax credits).

Financial problems are also linked to physical and mental health problems. For example, research has found that:

- 38% of those with moderate depression are in arrears
- 27% of those who have had suicidal thoughts in the past year are in arrears
- 49% of those with moderate or severe alcohol dependence are in arrears.[17]

The impact of debt is illustrated by quotes included in a study on living on a low income, and drawn from a range of qualitative studies:[18]

"Not being able to sleep, that's what gets me… At night when they're in bed, you start thinking, 'how am I going to pay this or that?' [The doctor] gave me some [sleeping] tablets but I daren't take them, couldn't wake up next morning and I'm scared if I don't hear the bairns in the night. Anyway, I don't need tablets, I need two hundred pounds."

"I was missing this and trying to avoid that and, in the end, I just didn't know where to turn… and the more [debt] I got into the more my mental health deteriorated… until I was admitted to hospital as a suicide risk."

Other research illustrates the impact of debt on long-term illness.[19] However, it is difficult to disentangle and explain the relationship between debt and health problems. Debt can clearly cause anxiety and stress, particularly when parents struggle to protect children from the full impact of inadequate material resources.[20, 21, 22] But health problems can also cause people to have money problems (eg, through job loss). So the direction of causation is unclear, as is the exact mechanism at work.

Financial capability and individual attitudes

In the last few years, government policy interest has turned to the issue of 'financial capability' with a concern that some people may not be sufficiently competent in relation to financial matters. The Introduction to the Financial Services Authority's (FSA's) recent survey, *Financial Capability in the UK: Delivering Change* (2006), claims: "Many people, particularly the young, are poorly equipped to plan ahead, and need to be significantly better at understanding the choices available to them."

In some ways, this echoes a long-standing stereotype: that people in poverty are poor money managers or even deliberately feckless, borrowing money recklessly and spending their money on inappropriate items. While it is certainly true that people on low incomes, like other groups, vary in the way they approach money management, and some may be 'better' money managers than others, there is considerable research evidence to suggest that, overall, people in poverty manage their finances with care, skill and resourcefulness. There is no evidence to suggest that there are two types of poor families – those who can cope and those who can't.[23]

Indeed, a recent survey on financial capability published by the FSA shows that while respondents on higher incomes were, unsurprisingly, more likely to make ends meet than those on lower incomes, "those on lower incomes scored more highly on keeping track of their money than respondents in the higher income groups".[24] Lone parents were among those doing best at keeping track of their money.

An analysis of the British Social Attitudes Survey found few differences in people's attitudes and behaviour to saving and spending by income level.[25] There was no evidence to suggest the existence of a 'feckless' poor who had particularly casual attitudes to debt; in fact, those on lower incomes were the most likely to take the view that 'people should never borrow money'. Similarly, there was no difference in attitudes towards the principle of whether people should spend or save when they are young.

People living in poverty generally deploy complex strategies to try to make ends meet but this does not necessarily enable them to manage on an insufficient income. A study in 1994 identified two different strategies: keeping tight control over finances; and living from day-to-day and paying the most pressing bill first.[26] Both strategies placed considerable strain on families, particularly mothers, who were categorised as being in one of the following groups:

- keeping heads above water
- struggling to the surface
- sinking
- drowning.

Although there will, of course, be some people on low incomes who are poor money managers (just as there are among more affluent groups), the evidence is clear that the majority of those in poverty simply do not have enough money to go round without either falling behind with commitments, borrowing money (often at high rates of interest, causing further strain when making repayments) and/or struggling to juggle their finances. Researchers often point to the resilience and resourcefulness of people in poverty. But it has been pointed out that countless studies warn about the "danger of painting too rosy a picture of women's resourcefulness that ignores the strain that it places on many of them".[27, 28]

Conclusion

Debt has increased most rapidly among higher-income groups, but it is generally lower-income families that face the most difficulties in keeping up with debt repayments. Families with children, lone parents in particular, are most likely to have debt problems. These families also, not surprisingly, find it difficult to save. Without a cushion of savings to help deal with dips in income, even small changes in circumstances can make debt unmanageable. The causes and consequences of debt are complex but it is clear that debt problems can lead to physical and mental health problems. Debt problems certainly place great strain on parents, particularly mothers, who generally manage their finances with care, skill and resourcefulness.

Notes

[1] Department of Trade and Industry, *Tackling Over-indebtedness*, Annual report 2006, DTI, London, 2006.

[2] R Lister, 'Poverty, material insecurity, and income vulnerability: the role of savings' in S Sodha and R Lister (eds) *The Saving Gateway: From Principles to Practice*, IPPR, London, 2006.

[3] S McKay and S Collard, 'Debt and financial exclusion' in C Pantazis, D Gordon and R Levitas (eds) *Poverty and Social Exclusion in Britain*, The Policy Press, Bristol, 2006.

[4] E Kempson, S McKay and M Willitts, *Characteristics of Families in Debt and the Nature of Indebtedness*, Department for Work and Pensions (DWP) Research Report no. 211, Corporate Document Services (CDS), Leeds, 2004.

[5] E Kempson, *Over-indebtedness in Britain*, DTI, London, 2002.

[6] A Del-Río and G Young, *The Impact of Unsecured Debt on Financial Distress among British Households*, Working Paper no. 262, Bank of England, London, 2005.

[7] McKay and Collard, 2006 (see note 3).

[8] E Kempson, 'Life on a low income: an overview of research on budgeting, credit and debt among the financially excluded' in Economic and Social Research Council, Swindon (ed) *How People on Low Incomes Manage their Finances*, ESRC, 2002.

[9] J Westaway and S McKay, *Women's Financial Assets and Debts*, Fawcett Society, London, 2007.

[10] C Emmerson and M Wakefield, *The Saving Gateway and the Child Trust Fund: Is asset-based welfare 'well fair'?*, Institute for Fiscal Studies, London, 2001.

[11] Kempson, 2002 (see note 8).

[12] McKay and Collard, 2006 (see note 3).

[13] S McKay and E Kempson, *Savings and Life Events*, DWP Research Report no. 194, CDS, Leeds 2003.

[14] McKay and Kempson, 2003 (see note 13).

[15] R Berthoud and E Kempson, *Credit and Debt: The PSI Survey*, Policy Studies Institute (PSI), London, 1992.

[16] Kempson *et al*, 2004 (see note 4).

[17] McKay and Collard, 2006 (see note 3).

[18] E Kempson, *Life on a Low Income*, Joseph Rowntree Foundation, York, 1996, pp. 45–46.

[19] N Balmer, P Pleasence, A Buck and H Walker, 'Worried Sick: The Experience of Debt Problems and their Relationship with Health, Illness and Disability', *Social Policy and Society*, 5 (2006), pp. 39–51.

[20] S Middleton, K Ashworth and I Braithwaite, *Small Fortunes: Spending on children, childhood poverty and parental sacrifice*, Joseph Rowntree Foundation, York, 1997.

[21] J Goode, C Callender and R Lister, *Purse or Wallet?*, PSI, London, 1998.

[22] C Farrell and W O'Connor, *Low-income Families and Household Spending*, DWP, CDS, Leeds, 2003.

[23] R Vaitilingam, Executive Summary in *How People on Low-incomes Manage their Finances*, Swindon: Economic and Social Research Council 2002, p. 4.

[24] A Atkinson, S McKay, E Kempson and S Collard, *Levels of Financial Capability in the UK: Results of a baseline survey*, FSA, London, 2006, p. 57.

[25] K Rowlingson and S McKay, 'Buy now, pay later?', in A Park, J Curtice, K Thomson, L Jarvis and C Bromley (eds) *British Social Attitudes Survey 19th Report*, Sage, London, 2002.

[26] E Kempson, A Bryson and K Rowlingson, *Hard Times? How poor families make ends meet*, PSI, London, 1994.

[27] Lister, 2006 (see note 2).

[28] Kempson 1996, p. 24 (see note 18).

7 The poverty premium

Claire Kober

Introduction

It has long been recognised that poverty brings with it a range of social penalties; low status, exclusion and isolation are all central to our understanding of the nature of deprivation and its effects.[1] However, there has been less recognition of the financial penalties associated with living in poverty. These penalties can restrict choice and result in those on low incomes paying a premium for a range of basic essentials.

The 'poverty premium' is the notional amount of additional money that a low-income household pays for essential goods and services. Those on a low income face this premium either because of the way they pay for services (for example, paying by cash or cheque as opposed to direct debit) or because of the way they buy (such as making use of 'pay as you go' options, which make budgeting easier but have a premium attached to them). Low-income consumers may also pay more because they are deemed to represent a higher risk – either directly or indirectly – to service providers. The result is that low-income consumers pay a premium of about £1,000 a year in acquiring cash and credit, and in purchasing goods and services.[2]

Policy-makers expend considerable amounts of time and energy exploring how best to get more money into the pockets of low-income families. Yet it is remarkable that little time is spent considering the unequal way in which money comes out of the pockets of these families.

This chapter considers the ways in which those on low incomes pay more across a range of sectors. It illustrates the limited choices available and the significant costs incurred by low-income consumers. It concludes by making a series of recommendations designed to improve the current situation. These should form an important part of any anti-poverty strategy.

Financial services

For most people financial services are an essential part of modern life: banks provide us with instant access to cash; debit and credit cards enable us to take advantage of online deals; and low-interest overdrafts help to tide us over when the end of the month approaches and cash flow becomes tight. However, a significant minority of families lack access to basic financial services; some 800,000 children live in households where nobody has a bank account[3] and two-thirds of households with no bank account have an annual income of under £14,500.[4]

Consumers who do not have a bank account are financially excluded and penalised in a number of ways: many employers require wages to be paid into a bank account, which leaves the unbanked at risk of exploitation in the informal economy; opportunities to borrow can be severely limited; and it may be difficult to build up assets. A simple action such as cashing a cheque, which is free of charge for most people with a bank account, often incurs significant fees for unbanked consumers, who have little option but to make use of high-cost cheque-cashing facilities.

In an investigation of the home credit market the Competition Commission found that there are around 400 cheque-cashers operating in the UK with 1,500 high street outlets.[5]

£200 cheque	
Paid into a bank account	Free
Cashed at Cash Converters (fee + 6%)	£16.50

Affordable credit

When people need extra money to cope with an unexpected cost there is a range of options available for those on average incomes. Affordable credit is taken for granted by many of us and provides a financial buffer against a range of short-term contingencies, both expected and unexpected. However, around 7.8 million adults across the UK do not have access to affordable credit, and options for this group are both limited and costly.[6]

People on low incomes needing cash urgently often resort to payday advance services. These services provide short-term loans; customers write a personal cheque to the lender and receive a cash sum. The lender waits for an agreed period – typically up to 30 days – before presenting the cheque to the bank. This is an expensive option and charges are often equivalent to an extremely high annual percentage rate (APR).

Payday loan

£300 loan (paid back 30 days later in a single payment)[7]   £375

The home credit market

Home credit or doorstep lenders, which typically offer small value, short-term unsecured loans, remain popular with many people on low incomes. A recent investigation by the Competition Commission found that the home credit market lent £1.3 billion to 2.3 million customers in 2005 and APRs were generally in excess of 100% and often above 300%.[8] Consumers who favour this option generally value the ability to borrow small amounts, the affordability of weekly repayments and the home collection feature that ensures that they do not miss payments.

Provident Financial, which represents more than 50% of the home credit market, has recently launched a sub-prime credit card, the Provident Visa Card, aimed at its home credit customers. The card is available in values of £300 and operates like a debit card in the sense that customers cannot go over an agreed limit. Payments are managed in the same way as home credit loans, with an agent collecting repayments each week from the customer's home. The card, which also allows cash withdrawals, attracts an APR of 183.2%.[9]

Cost of borrowing £300 on a credit card

From typical credit card
(15% APR paid over 56 weeks)   £325.20

From a Provident Visa Card
(183.2% APR paid over 56 weeks)   £504.00

Rental purchase shops

When there is a need to meet a hefty cost, low-income consumers often have little choice but to make use of sub-prime rental purchase shops. These shops are a common feature of high streets in deprived neighbourhoods. The market leader is BrightHouse, which boasts more than 150 stores. Stores such as BrightHouse are an attractive option to those on low incomes, as they do not carry out any credit checks. Instead, customers are required give the name of four friends or family members who are willing to act as referees.

Goods in BrightHouse carry both high APRs and high mark-ups on retail prices. For example, BrightHouse is currently selling a washing machine, which is available from Sainsbury's for £336, that can be paid for over 156 weeks at a total cost of £606.84. On top of the basic cost, customers are encouraged to take out 'optional service cover' that provides the opportunity to take a payment holiday of up to 12 months or return a product at any time without penalty should they decide they no longer want it or are unable to afford repayments. Most customers sign up for this option, which, in the case of the washing machine in question, adds an additional £2.10 to the weekly repayment rate, meaning that the total amount payable increases to £934.44.

A recent addition to the sub-prime credit sector is to be found in the form of a company called Log Book Loans. Borrowers are required to deposit their car log book with the company and in return are provided with a cash loan. The car log book is essentially used as security for the loan; customers retain the use of their car but they are prevented from selling it. Loans attract a typical APR of 343.4%. A commitment fee of £215, repaid throughout the term of the loan, is also payable on all loans and included in the weekly repayment fee.

Cost of borrowing £1,500

From typical bank (19% APR over 52 weeks)	£1,646.16
From Log Book Loans (343.4% APR + £215 commitment fee over 58 weeks)	£3,120.40

Insurance

As insurers' ability to assess risk becomes more sophisticated, people on low incomes, who are more likely to live in areas with higher property and car crime, often face higher insurance premiums than people who live in more affluent areas. The effect of this is that low-income consumers are considerably less likely to have insurance cover than those on higher incomes; nearly half of all households in the poorest fifth of the population do not have home contents insurance.[10]

Many household insurers continue to insist that policyholders insure for high minimum values, often well beyond the value of goods owned by people on low incomes. Similarly, most insurers require customers to pay via direct debit or other methods that require a bank account. Industry representatives argue that this is because of difficulties in collecting payments efficiently from people without bank accounts; the impact is to reduce the availability of cover for those on a low income.

Conclusion and recommendations

Poverty sharply limits the choices available to consumers and leaves them with little option but to make short-term decisions at the expense of longer-term financial stability. A family's inability to pay an unexpected bill one day might force them to secure a high-interest doorstep loan the next, or to resort to pawnbrokers and buy-back stores. The reality is that many low-income families are making use of the only options available to them when they take out a payday loan, make use of doorstep lenders or replace essential household goods through rental purchase stores.

So what can be done to eradicate the poverty premium to ensure that those on the lowest incomes do not pay more for life's essentials? In some areas there is clearly a role for government and regulators to take action to ensure equity of access. In others, when the market fails, central and local government need to consider the possibility of becoming providers of low-cost services; 'insurance with rent' schemes,[11] provided by local authorities to extend access to insurance for social housing tenants, are proof that this is possible. Finally, there is a need to think creatively about the role of social enterprise in filling gaps in the market and developing new models of provision.

It is often said that the first step to changing something is to measure it. It is estimated that the poverty premium could account for nearly 10% of a poor family's income after housing costs.[12] Yet the government does not currently measure the extent of the poverty premium or how it is changing over time. This means there is no official understanding of the extent to which it diminishes family incomes. The government should commit itself to producing a Poverty Premium Index, similar to the Retail Prices Index, to track changes in the prices of a basket of essential goods and services. As the Retail Prices Index is often used as the basis for wage negotiations, so the Poverty Premium Index should be used to inform benefit uprating decisions.

Beyond these broad recommendations, there are a number of specific steps that could be taken to tackle the poverty premium:

- Regulators should provide customers with standardised price comparison information to ensure that all consumers are alert to the potential benefits of switching network providers. This information is already available to energy customers but needs to spread to other sectors.
- While significant progress has been made on the financial exclusion agenda in recent years, there remains much to be done to ensure full financial inclusion for all consumers.
- Access to free, independent financial advice needs to be available to all. Improving access to advice would not only benefit individuals, who would better understand their options and entitlements, but by improving financial literacy, would have knock-on benefits for government and the financial services industry.
- Many of the most vulnerable consumers are pushed towards high-cost and illegal borrowing options as a direct result of the failings of the government's own financial safety net, the Social Fund. Radical reform of the Social Fund is now long overdue. A fund with wider eligibility criteria, far more cash available, more flexible repayment terms, and less stigma in the way it functions could make a real contribution to tackling the poverty premium.

Notes

[1] See, for example, P Townsend, *Poverty in the UK*, Allen Lane. Harmondsworth, 1979.

[2] Save the Children/Family Welfare Association, *The Poverty Premium: How poor households pay more for essential goods and services*, 2007.

[3] HM Treasury, *Financial Inclusion: Credit, savings, advice and insurance*, Treasury Select Committee, 12th report of the session 2005/06.

[4] HM Treasury, *Promoting Financial Inclusion*, 2004.

[5] Competition Commission, *Home Credit Market Investigation*, 2006.

[6] National Consumer Council, *Affordable Credit: A model that recognises real needs*, 2005.

[7] www.paydayuk.co.uk. This is equivalent to an APR of 1,355%.

[8] Competition Commission, 2006 (see note 5).

[9] http://www.providentpersonalcredit.com/products/VisaCard.aspx

[10] Joseph Rowntree Foundation, *Monitoring Poverty and Social Exclusion*, 2005.

[11] 'Insurance with rent' schemes are often run by local authorities or housing associations and exist to encourage the purchase of insurance by enabling home contents insurance for local authority tenants to be paid for along with rent.

[12] Save the Children/Family Welfare Association, 2007 (see note 2).

Part 2

Poverty: the impact on wellbeing

8 Childhood poverty and life chances

Paul Gregg

Introduction

We know from existing research and indeed the other chapters in this volume that children from poorer backgrounds do less well in a number of dimensions than their peers. There is also recent evidence that the relationship between family incomes and children's outcomes increased for children born in 1970 compared with those born in 1958.[1] Evidence suggests that this was largely a consequence of an increased relationship between family income and educational attainment.[2]

The extent to which poor attainment is caused by low income is, however, less clear. Low-income families have many disadvantages, the parents are generally less well educated and often younger, and families are often larger. All of these family factors may well still lead to lower attainment even if incomes were to rise substantially. The fundamental question is whether it is money itself that makes the difference to children's lives and opportunities. However, there are clearly mechanisms by which income can directly influence attainment, such as childcare quality, resources in the home environment, family stress, social activities, neighbourhoods and the schools children attend. If these are important, then increasing income inequality will translate into inequalities in children's educational outcomes and their life chances. A clearer understanding of these issues is key to appreciating the extent to which goals of equality of opportunity can be reconciled with wide income inequalities, and they are essential to evaluating the educational benefits of reducing child poverty. To isolate the impact of income alone is not straightforward and so this chapter will be quite technical in places.

It is useful to start thinking about what we need to understand. Family income at a point in time can be thought of as a combination of average income through the childhood years plus any temporary deviation that occurs at any particular point in time, and in addition there is likely to be some mis-measurement in any data used. Any mis-measurement introduces noise into any study of income and education attainment, leading to understatement of the true effects. Furthermore, families are likely to respond to temporary changes in income through loss of a job or a few hours' overtime rather differently than they respond to long-term income differences. For instance, families will not move house to get close to a good school, or build an extension so a child has its own workspace, or buy a car to have access to a wider set of activities. As income averaged over several years will have less measurement error, this might suggest that long-term income should be the focus of any study of income on outcomes. However, other aspects of deprivation such as low parental education are strongly related to long-term income. Hence, a simple study of long-term low income on child outcomes will mix up the effect of money with all the other differences between families to a greater extent for long-term income than for temporary income.

So there are two major problems to be concerned about. First, income, especially long-term income, is associated with lots of other family differences that themselves make a difference to children's life chances. Second, poor measurement of income and temporary income shocks will lead to an understating of the true effect of long-term income differences on children's outcomes. To overcome these problems economists and social researchers have tried a number of approaches. Over the last ten years or so research from the USA has used a variety of methods of controlling for family background and heterogeneity, and it finds that family income does have a direct positive effect on educational attainment. However, there is substantial variation in the strength of the identified effect. This chapter will explain these approaches and will attempt to explore them with British data where possible and, where not, will discuss the North American data in detail.

We begin this section by estimating some basic models of how income and educational attainment are related in three time periods, using data from the National Child Development Survey (NCDS), when the children were aged 16 in 1974; British Cohort Study (BCS), 1986; and British Household Panel Survey (BHPS), 1975–80. Table 1 is based on research published in Blanden and Gregg (2004).[3] We then control for a series of family characteristics, such as parental education, in order to show the extent to which the patterns are modified by the most straightforward attempts to reduce bias. The first panel

Table 1: Relationship between qualifications and income at age 16

Impact of one-third lower income (£7,500) at age 16 from ordered probit models			
A. No controls	(1) NCDS 1958	(2) BCS 1970	(3) BHPS 1975–80
No A–C GCSEs	+8.1% ***	+9.6% ***	+5.7%***
Degree attainment	-4.0% ***	-07.4% ***	-8.7%***
Specification conditions for basic demographics and parents' education	(7) NCDS 1958	(8) BCS 1970	(9) BHPS 1975–80
No A-C GCSEs	+5.7% ***	+7.1% ***	+4.3% ***
Degree attainment	-2.8% ***	-5.6% ***	-6.7% ***
Sample size	7,138	4,708	580

Notes:
1. The dependent variable is highest qualification which is coded as (1) "No qualifications, or qualifications below GCSE A–C or equivalent"; (2) "GCSE A–C or equivalent"; (3) "A level or equivalent"; (4) "Degree or equivalent". For the NCDS this variable is measured at age 33, for the BCS at age 30 and for the BCS age 23 (or 22 if this is not available).
2. Basic demographic controls are the child's sex, ethnicity, dummies for number of siblings in the household and controls for parents' age group. In all the BHPS specifications controls are added for the wave in which the child is 16.
3. Marginal effects are calculated as the average impact of a .4 reduction in log income, which is approximately one-third reduction in the level of income. This is £98 at the mean for the NCDS, £96 at the mean for the BCS and £140 at the mean for the BHPS.

in Table 1 presents results showing the raw association between family income at age 16 and qualifications, with no controls added. In order to ease interpretation, effects are calculated to show the change in probability of obtaining the lowest and highest qualification category in response to a one-third reduction in income for a typical-income family (the median family).

The raw effect of reducing income by one-third is to increase the chance of obtaining no GCSEs A–C or equivalent by 6 to 9 percentage points, depending on the cohort used, and the probability of obtaining a degree by

4 to 9 percentage points. There is therefore *prima facie* evidence of the attainment gap shifting from the lower levels of qualifications to the higher education level as educational attainment generally rose in the population.

Evidence from the UK indicates that low income has an independent effect on children's outcomes after controlling for key aspects of family background and children's measured ability.[4] In the lower panel, controls for family background (the child's sex, family size, parental age and race) and parental education are added. The implied income relationships are reduced by about one-fifth to a quarter. So with these controls included, the income effects remain strong and the patterns over time are unchanged. Here a one-third drop in income led to a 3 to 7 point fall in the probability of obtaining a degree. However, to be confident that the effect of income has been accurately isolated requires more than controlling for some easily observed aspects of family background. It is highly likely that there are unobserved child or family characteristics that differ between more and less affluent families that will still lead to an overstatement of the extent to which money drives child attainment.

Alternative strategies

Disentangling income effects from difficult-to-observe family or child differences requires some ingenuity. The most frequently used type of approach exploits variations in incomes within families, rather than longer-term income differences that may have larger effects.[5] So it is this approach that is studied first. In this broad approach the idea is to focus on changes in income. The argument is that long-term income differences between families are closely related to other differences across families, such as parental education, number of siblings or parenting styles. However, this approach will understate the effects of income if transitory income has smaller effects than long-term income, and in these approaches measurement error in the data becomes more problematic as year-to-year changes in income become very noisy. There are a number of variations in this approach. Sibling studies look at how siblings growing up in the same family will often experience different family incomes when at the same age. So, for example, an older child was aged 16 in a period when there is no available overtime work in the father's job, but this was not so for the younger one. This variation in income when the children are the same age then can be linked to children's development while living with same parents, etc. So the argument goes: the income is what lies behind any differences in children's achievement. The central problem for sibling studies is that siblings will often be close in age, and experience very similar income patterns for most of their childhood. Also, only families with two or more children can be considered.

The second approach in this set controls for income observed in the same family after the child has finished full-time education. This income cannot have an impact on the child's earlier attainment but will reflect long-term income of the parents. So by netting out long-term parental income we observe the relationship between temporarily high or low income in (normally late) childhood impacts on child development. In a similar vein an individual child's development can be tracked between two dates, and how development varies across children be compared with how income varied in these families, so the impact of changes in income on changes in child development are considered.

Looking at differences between siblings as income affects their development is not easy in the UK, as few studies follow siblings long term. The one study that does this, the British Household Panel Survey, has few participants in any year, so we have to pool a number of years to explore a number of years, and the need to observe both siblings completing their education makes the numbers observed very small. Comparing differences in income between siblings at the age of 18 reduces the degree attainment gap to -3.3 percentage points for a one-third income drop. However, the small sample makes the estimate imprecise.

The second approach to net out long-term income is control for income after the child has completed education. This approach can only be applied to the UK using the BHPS again. This approach of including family income when the child is aged around 21 makes little additional difference to just conditioning on family demographics and parental education (shown in Table 1). The third approach is to focus on changes in income and attainment for each child, exploring what happens to a child's educational development as income rises faster or falls relative to other families. The results suggest that a one-third reduction in income increases the propensity to achieve no A–C GCSEs by just over 3 percentage points, and has a similar magnitude reduction in the propensity to get a degree.

In summary, models that explore temporary income changes on children's attainment give rather smaller estimates than those that include only controls for family characteristics. The range is for estimates that a one-third reduction in family income raises the probability of getting no A–C GCSEs by about 3 to 4 percentage points, and the probability of attending university is reduced by between 3 and 6 percentage points. So they suggest that the causal impact of income on attainment is about one-third of the actual differences observed between more and less affluent children. The recurring problem with these forms of estimation is that by relying on temporary differences in income within families, plus the effect of measurement error, mean that the results of these models can be considered the smallest plausible size of the impact on children's attainment.

Experimental trials of policy interventions

In the USA there have been a number of welfare-to-work programmes undertaken under experimental conditions, and evidence from these is perhaps the cleanest and clearest available. The relevant population in the trial is divided into a treated group who participate in the programme and an untreated control group. Some welfare reforms that focus on getting lone mothers into employment (and off welfare) have included child outcomes in their evaluations. The most comprehensive assessment of the effects on children is contained in Clark-Kauffman *et al* (2003);[6] we report the key results from this paper in Table 2.

This analysis pools the data from a large number of random assignment welfare experiments and compares the treated and control groups. These programmes were aiming to raise employment and earnings of welfare-dependent families in the USA; some also offered additional cash assistance when mothers moved into work. Column 1 reports the evidence of programme effects on child educational attainment test scores for those programmes with cash assistance, so that the observed changes in child outcomes reflect the combined effect of work and income changes. The income gains among the treated participants in these earnings-supplement programmes were modest, at $1,500–$2,000 (£1,000 to £1,300 at Purchasing Power Parity rates) per year over the untreated participants for two to three years. Column 2 shows the impact on child test scores for programmes based on raising maternal employment without additional in-work financial support. These had positive employment and earnings effects but had very modest effects on family incomes, as benefit payments are withdrawn. The differences between columns 1 and 2 reflect the impact of the extra effect of income, as both types of programmes led to similar

Table 2: The impact on test scores of welfare to work; results from experimental evaluations

Treatment age	Treatment effects on test scores	
	(1) Earnings-supplement programmes	(2) All other programmes
Age 0–2	0.082** (0.034)	-0.016 (0.074)
Age 3–5	0.080** (0.026)	0.035 (0.026)
Age 6–8	-0.025 (0.033)	-0.015 (0.070)
Age 9–11	-0.043 (0.040)	-0.046 (0.082)
Age 12–15	-0.039 (0.060)	-0.167 (0.102)
R-squared	.0346	.0409
Observations	18,641	11,982

Notes:

1. Source: Clark-Kauffman *et al* (2003), Table 1.[7]
2. The dependent variable is a within-study standardised measure of attainment; the precise nature of this varies by the study and in some cases more than one measure is provided.
3. Controls are included in all models for follow-up length, prior earnings, prior earnings squared, prior welfare receipt (AFDC benefits), prior years of employment, high school degree, teen parent, marital status, number of children and age of youngest child.
4. Dummies are also added for the type of achievement measure and the study that the data are taken from.
5. ** Statistically significant at the 5% level.

employment and earnings changes. The size of the attainment gains for preschool children is modest, but statistically significant, with test scores up by 8% of a standard deviation. At older ages there are no differences across the programmes except that at ages 12 to 15 there are large, but poorly identified, negative results associated with the programmes without earnings supplement.

This is very clear evidence of income effects for those aged under 6 and of similar magnitude, but less clear (statistically speaking), income effects for teenagers. However, this evidence is limited to small income gains for low-income lone-parent families and it is not clear how this would translate to wider populations.

While money is rarely given randomly via experiments, income shocks do occur naturally through economic recessions or tax and welfare changes. Dahl and Lochner (2005)[8] explore the impact of income changes resulting from the US Earned Income Tax Credit (EITC). They suggest that an extra $1,000 a year in tax credits over three years raises reading and maths scores by about 3% of a standard deviation. This appears similar to the experimental evidence described above but averaged over all school-age children. They also suggest that the effect is larger for poorer families. As these estimates are derived from a large range of family incomes, we can compare these estimates with UK data. They suggest that a family with £7,800 annual higher income for three years would achieve 30% of a standard deviation higher in tests. Using Key Stage 2 tests as a benchmark, one-third of a standard deviation is 1.5 KS2 points, which is about half of the gap between free school meals children and the rest at age 11.

In a similar vein, Gregg *et al* (2007)[9] look at the impact of the working families' tax credit (WFTC) on lone parents and their children, but they do not consider educational outcomes, as not enough children have reached age 16 as yet in the BHPS. However, they report that lone mothers saw sharp reductions in adverse mental health outcomes (eg, depression) shortly after the WFTC kicked in, when compared with other women living without partners (who did not receive WFTC). This improved mental wellbeing was strongly associated with reduced financial stress.

Teenage children in the BHPS report on a number of outcomes ranging from personal unhappiness on a range of issues, relationships within the family and engaging in certain risky behaviours. Children of lone parents report higher levels of unhappiness about school work, about their family and about life as a whole. On all these measures the gaps diminished after the WFTC was introduced, raising family income.

Reported relationships between child and mother improved. Children of lone parents report playing truant and smoking more often and are more often suspended from school and intending to leave school at age 16 compared with children living with two parents, although they are not more likely to be involved in fights. After the WFTC was introduced there was a marked narrowing in these gaps for playing truant and smoking. Perhaps most relevant here is that those reporting they intended to leave school at age 16 fell by 5 percentage points among teenagers of lone parents compared with just 1.6% in the case of children living with two parents. The impact of WFTC on lone parents came not just through direct transfer of money; the same study shows that WFTC induced 5% of lone mothers to move into work, and with the increased earnings those with children under 12 saw their real incomes rise by as much as 18%.

Conclusions

This chapter discusses evidence about whether there is a causal impact of family income on educational attainment and, if so, how large the effect is. The evidence clearly indicates that there exists an important causal relationship between family income and educational attainment of children in the UK. The study of the impact of the WFTC suggests that children's behaviours, happiness and family functioning all improved for lone parents after its introduction, as did mothers' depression levels. Increasing financial resources for lone parents has far wider effects than just educational attainment.

We first summarise the evidence from approaches that focus on transitory income shocks to isolate causal effects from money on child attainment. These net out the relationship between long-term income and family characteristics (such as parental education) suggesting that a one-third reduction in family income from the mean, which is about £150 a week or £7,800 a year, reduces the chances of securing a degree by around 3 to 4 percentage points. Effects of a similar magnitude are found for the other outcomes we consider – obtaining no GCSE A–C grades and staying on at school. These approaches suggest that around one third of educational attainment deficits of poor children come from lack of financial resources. However, as discussed, these should be considered lower bound estimates.

Alternative approaches that focus on changes in long-term income that come from policy changes (such as EITC in the USA, akin to WFTC in UK) or experimental interventions suggest larger effects. Applying these estimates to the UK would suggest that an income loss of £7,800 a year (a one-third cut for the typical family) would result in closing half of the attainment gap between free school meal children and typical children.

A natural question to ask is whether this is a large impact or not, especially as £7,800 sounds like a large change to annual incomes compared with the 4 to 6 percentage point change in outcomes it leads to. So, in order to bring this into focus, the estimates suggest that around 50% of educational inequality we observe in the UK, the gaps in attainment between rich and poor, stem from differences in income. These results demonstrate that when combined with substantial income inequality, the impact of income has important implications for educational inequality.

From a policy point of view £7,800 a year is a large amount of money, far beyond the income redistribution that is likely to be achieved by taxes and benefits. However, a broader attempt to reduce the inequalities in the distribution of work and wages offers hope of more substantial progress. The WFTC made a much larger impact on incomes than just the cash spent, as increased employment added considerable extra family earnings. In addition, direct interventions to raise attainment of those from poorer families, through early years education and extra resources for schools, can be cost-effective if they are well targeted. Recent government policy seems to be making a concerted effort to address these issues with continued financial redistribution to families and education investments ranging from preschool programmes through to raising the school leaving age. It is for future research to discover whether these attempts are successful in creating greater equality of opportunity.

Notes

[1] J Blanden, P Gregg, A Goodman and S Machin, *Changes in Intergenerational Mobility in Britain*, Centre for the Economics of Education Discussion Paper no.26, London School of Economics, 2002 and forthcoming in M Corak (ed) *Generational Income Mobility in North America and Europe*, Cambridge University Press.

[2] J Blanden, P Gregg and L Macmillan, 'Accounting for intergenerational income persistence: Non-cognitive skills, ability and education', *Economic Journal*, no. 117, March 2007, C43–60.

[3] J Blanden and P Gregg, 'Family income and educational attainment: A review of approaches and evidence for Britain', *Oxford Review of Economic Policy*, vol. 20 no. 2, June 2004.

[4] See P Gregg and S Machin, 'Childhood Disadvantage and Success or Failure in the Labour Market', in D Blanchflower and R Freeman (eds) *Youth Employment and Joblessness in Advanced Countries*, National Bureau of Economic Research, Cambridge, MA, 2000, and J Hobcraft, *Intergenerational and life-course transmission of social exclusion: Influences and childhood poverty, family disruption and contact with the police*, CASE Paper no. 15, Centre for Analysis of Social Exclusion, London School of Economics, 1998.

[5] See, for example, S Mayer, *What Money Can't Buy: Family Income and Children's Life Chances*, Harvard University Press, Cambridge, MA, 1998, or D Levy and G Duncan, *Using Siblings to Assess the Effect of Childhood Family Income on Completed Schooling*, Joint Center for Poverty Research Working Paper, Northwestern University, Evanston, IL, 2000.

[6] E Clark-Kauffman, G Duncan and P Morris, 'How Welfare Policies Affect Child and Adolescent Achievement', *American Economic Review*, 93 (2003), pp. 299–303.

[7] See note 6.

[8] G B Dahl and L Lochner, *The Impact of Family Income on Child Achievement*, NBER Working Papers 11279, National Bureau of Economic Research, Inc., 2005.

[9] P Gregg, S Harkness and S Smith (2007) *Welfare Reform and Lone Parents in the UK*, Centre for Market and Public Organisation, Discussion Paper no. 182, 2007.

9 The psychology of poverty

Wendy Wrapson, Avril J Mewse and Stephen E G Lea

Poverty as a psychological condition

Poverty is an economic, social and psychological condition. It is not as obvious as it might seem precisely what that condition is: the definition of poverty occupies a large section of any academic treatment of the subject. One reason for this is that poverty means different things within the discourse of different academic disciplines, and economists, sociologists and psychologists are likely to find different definitions helpful. In reflecting on the psychological aspects of poverty, however, we need to avoid getting involved in this debate. Our opening statement, that poverty is in part a psychological condition, may strike some readers as strange. Economic and social factors set broad boundary conditions but we argue that psychological responses to these conditions can make both objective and subjective differences to the likely outcomes for people living in poverty. It is prudent at this point to clarify that we are talking about the psychology of poverty in rich countries. It is important to be clear about this because traditional economies, where poverty is the typical condition, and modern developed economies, where poverty is a minority condition, produce very different psychologies.[1]

The psychology of poverty is not particularly deep or subtle. There is no need for elaborate psychological theory about how people feel when living in poverty. The feeling of poverty has social and economic causes and consequences. However, there may be psychological reasons why people fall within the social and economic boundary conditions for poverty, and psychological processes that either keep them there or help them escape. In understanding what happens to people who are within the zone of potential poverty in a rich society, and in observing their distinctive behaviour and predicting its consequences, an economically informed psychology has much work to do. In our view, that work needs to be done from a particular standpoint. The sociological and economic literature on poverty has primarily been focused on quantitative analyses of what constitutes poverty and the prevalence of poverty. There has been far less work that has tried to understand what living in poverty means to an individual. Lea, Burgoyne, Jones and Beer (1997)[2] have noted previously that research on poverty has tended to be conducted *about* people living in poverty, rather than *by* or *with* them. Since then Bennett and Roberts (2004)[3] have provided an overview of participatory approaches to research into poverty and they highlight the importance of giving people with direct experience of poverty more voice in the research process, from defining the issues to working out potential solutions. Similarly, Ridge (2002)[4] in her examination of childhood poverty and social exclusion emphasised the importance of a deeper understanding of the lived experience of poverty in childhood. She pointed out that despite the considerable amount of quantitative data relating to childhood poverty, there is a dearth of meaningful qualitative data. Ridge reports findings from interviews with children and young people living in poverty (and with some of their parents) about issues and concerns that they identify as important. Although there has been an increase in recent years in participatory research projects, there are few such studies in the psychological literature. This point was highlighted recently by Underlid (2007),[5] who stressed the continuing need for research focusing on psychological issues and theoretical perspectives relating to the lived experience of poverty. The literature on people's individual experiences of poverty, although somewhat sparse, is the focus of this chapter.

Poverty as constraint

The beginning of a psychological analysis of poverty is to recognise that poverty is bound up with constraint. Resources are limited, and consumption for most people is limited by income constraints. But low income limits the choices available to people in all kinds of ways that are not typical of the general population. In interviews conducted by Lea *et al* (1997)[6] with people with severe financial difficulties, participants identified restrictions in choice about where they lived, the clothes they wore, the food they ate, and the daily activities they could undertake. As one single parent commented:

"I will probably have to manage on spuds for a week or something like that or bread, there is no other way of doing it. You just don't have enough. You can't

have luxuries really. You see I only get… and by the time I've paid for water, electric, TV, nappies and food there isn't much left for anything but I still got to get shampoo, soap, toothpaste for me, and things like that you know."

A consistent theme in interviews with people in poverty is their desire to ensure that, however limited their own lives are, their children should have the same opportunities as their peers. Parents often scrimp and save, going without themselves, to make sure they can not only provide for their children's basic needs but provide them with treats and presents.[7] Children nevertheless do often have to go without or 'make do'. For adults, having to wear old and second-hand clothing because they cannot afford new clothing gives a visible aspect to poverty and may make people more readily identifiable as members of a disadvantaged group.[8] For children this can seem particularly hard and it can lead to bullying and social exclusion.

Poverty can also mean that young people miss out on some aspects of childhood in less obviously financial ways. They may have additional family responsibilities and stresses compared with their peers. They may help to contribute to the family income, help care for younger brothers and sisters, and help look after parents with health problems.[9] Young people interviewed in a study conducted by Crowley and Vulliamy (2007)[10] described how they are often unable to afford to participate in social activities with their peers, which also reduces their social networks. As one young person noted, "When you haven't got much money – you miss out on life" (p. 13). One way of obtaining things they may not otherwise be able to afford is to turn to crime. Stealing may simply be a way of surviving, "Sometimes you have to steal to eat, if you're homeless or have nowhere to go" (p. 20). Other young people noted that desperation or feeling "worthless" may make people turn to drugs because this gave them something in their otherwise empty lives.

Coping strategies and coping failures

Much of the behaviour associated with poverty can also be understood within the context of constraint. People in poverty have multiple strategies for reducing the impact of poverty. These can be grouped into overcoming the practical problems of poverty (eg, managing on a low income), coping with the consequences of poverty (eg, the homeless may need to find somewhere to go during the day), and minimising the psychological impact of poverty (eg, seeing the situation as temporary so as to have hope for a better future).[11]

Budgeting is an important coping strategy for people living in poverty. However, for those on low incomes budgeting can be difficult. People often have to juggle their commitments and put off paying for certain items in order to meet their more urgent needs. To avoid debt they constantly have to prioritise which accounts should be paid first, although they are fairly consistent about which bills should be accorded the highest priorities.[12] Additional expenses that arise unexpectedly quickly throw financial management strategies out of kilter:

> "I think it is I am robbing Peter to pay Paul a lot of it, one week I will buy an expensive item, the next week I buy an expensive item. Loo rolls and bleach and washing-up liquid, washing powder – they seem the most expensive so I try and get it so I don't run out of two things in one week, or that's it, fatal."

Paying by easily accessible forms of credit, such as purchasing items through catalogue companies, is a common way of making money go further:[13]

> "... well this year is going to be the first time on my own and I will have to use the club-book probably, and pay it back for the rest of the year."

The psychological literature indicates that most consumers, faced with assessing credit offers, tend to regard the overall cost of an item as less important than the amount they must find weekly or monthly to service that cost.[14] For low-income families this factor becomes overwhelming, whether it is in connection with the acquisition of new goods or with the repayment of old debts. The effect is that they often pay a high total cost, further exacerbating their financial problems (see Chapter 7).

To help themselves cope with poverty, people may use strategies to maintain self-esteem, such as expressing pride in their success at budgeting or by ensuring that their children are well fed and clothed as far as resources allow, so that they can show they can take care of their child:[15]

> "I mean I am doing well, she is dressed well, she is clean, she is healthy, that is the main thing, know what I mean, she is not going round looking filthy, like some of the kids you see. So at least she is looked after... nobody can say I am not looking after her."

Poverty, psychological wellbeing and mental health

Despite people's efforts to buffer the impacts of poverty, economic hardship has an adverse effect on psychological wellbeing. Poverty is both a cause and a consequence of poor mental health. The causal relationships between poor mental health and poverty, deprivation and social exclusion are complex and not clearly understood (see Payne (1999).[16] For example, depression can onset as a result of experiencing poverty, perhaps as a consequence of unemployment; and conversely, poverty can be the result of episodic depression that has led to loss of work and perhaps housing. Although more research is needed to illustrate the causal pathways there is no doubt that adults in the poorest fifth of the population are twice as likely to develop a mental illness as those on average incomes.[17] Adults with a diagnosis of schizophrenia are concentrated in the lowest income groups, whereas their parents show a much more typical income distribution.[18] As indicated above, the effects of poverty on psychological wellbeing and mental health are not simple, and they vary depending on the setting (rural vs. urban), race, age and gender.[19] Furthermore, people living in poverty who have good relationships with their families may be buffered somewhat from the stresses and strains of their situation.[20] Good family relationships may make people living in poverty feel better valued, that their lives are more meaningful, and make them feel less hopeless about the future than those with poor family relationships. We have found that people who maintain good relationships with their family are able to call upon family members to help out in times of financial crisis.[21] When finances are dire, such help can be invaluable:

> "… and dad gave me £100 towards the stuff from the auction which was over £200 worth. OK, that was cooker, fridge-freezer, wall unit and small wardrobe and a couple of bedside cabinets… He gave me that and at the moment my mum is paying off my catalogue bill… My mum paid for the carpeting and I paid for the curtains and everything. Everything else I cover."

Is there a way out of poverty?

Is poverty episodic or persistent over the life course? In interviews with people in difficult financial circumstances, we have found that people often believe their financial status will change only if their circumstances change for the better – for example, through obtaining a decent job.[22] The expression of optimism about the future being dependent on external events has been shown in other studies.[23] People will also often say, however, that such an event is unlikely to happen, reflecting feelings of inadequacy or inability to control financial outcomes. This is not unexpected, given that attitudinal differences have been found between those in low and high income households. Hill *et al* (1985)[24] found correlations between earnings and family income and positive beliefs in personal efficacy and personal control. If people perceive they have little control over outcomes they may feel helpless to change their financial situation[25] and may believe they will never achieve financial security. Such beliefs are, to some extent, well founded. There is certainly little opportunity for people with low skill levels and low levels of education to increase their income; research has shown that mothers who leave the welfare system to work rarely manage to obtain a high-wage job.[26] However, such beliefs can have negative effects on strategies used to address poverty-driven debt. We found that people in debt who believed that they could eventually be debt-free were more likely to engage with creditors to discuss making payments than those who felt they could not become debt-free (Lea *et al*, in prep.).[27]

Poverty: more than a state of mind

Income matters. It is commonly reported that in a modern economy, people's happiness is not much correlated with their income, but there is an exception. At low levels of income, the correlation becomes both larger and more reliable.[28] At all levels of income, there are people who are more inclined than others to feel that their happiness depends on their material possessions, and such high-materialism individuals are less likely to be happy than their less materialistic peers.[29] But at low-income levels, even a relative disregard for material goods will not protect people against greater unhappiness.

It is one of the most pervading truths of psychology that people adapt to circumstances, whether at the lowest level of perception, or at the level of social situations such as powerlessness and poverty. We adapt in two ways: we stop noticing the absolute level of our condition, responding only to changes; and we do things that will tend to reinstate previous conditions. Faced with the constraints of poverty, people both become less sensitive to them and resist them with a variety of practical and psychological strategies.[30] But this does not mean that people living in poverty cease to be poor. As typically occurs in any physical, biological or social system, adaptation is not complete. People exposed to lower income than they need to maintain what society regards as a decent standard of living do put in place behavioural and psychological coping strategies, and these do mitigate some of the effects of shortage of money. But the equilibrium that is reached is at a lower level of quality of life, psychological wellbeing and general happiness than the majority of people in a rich society expect.

Notes

Research on which this chapter partly depends was supported by HM Courts Service for England.

Quotations were taken from a sample of interviews conducted with single parents for research reported in Lea, Burgoyne, Jones and Beer (1997); see note 2 below.

[1] S E G Lea and P Anand, 'The psychology and behavioural economics of poverty', in International Association for Research in Economic Psychology (ed), *Proceedings of the 32nd Symposium, Filozofska fakulteta, Ljubljana*, 2007, pp. 486–92; and see, for example, K Hundeide, 'Four different meanings of "being poor"', *Psychology and Developing Societies*, 11 (1999), pp. 143–55.

[2] S E G Lea, C B Burgoyne, S M Jones and A J Beer, 'An interview study of the psychology of Poverty' in International Association for Research in Economic Psychology (ed), *The XXII International Colloquium of Economic Psychology*, Valencia, Promolibro, Valencia, 1997, pp. 955–67.

[3] F Bennett and M Roberts, *From Input to Influence: Participatory approaches to research and inquiry into poverty*, Joseph Rowntree Foundation, York, 2004.

[4] T Ridge, *Childhood Poverty and Social Exclusion: From a child's perspective*, Policy Press, Bristol, 2002.

[5] K Underlid, 'Poverty and experiences of insecurity. a qualitative interview study of 25 long-standing recipients of social security, *International Journal of Social Welfare*, 16 (2007), pp. 65–74.

[6] See note 2.

[7] T Kochuyt, 'Giving away one's poverty. On the consumption of scarce resources within the family', *Sociological Review*, 52:2 (2004), pp. 139–61; S E G Lea, P Webley and C M Walker, 'Psychological factors in consumer debt: Money management, economic socialization, and credit use', *Journal of Economic Psychology*, 16 (1995), pp. 681–701.

[8] See note 2.

[9] D Roker and J Coleman, '"The invisible poor": Young people growing up in family poverty', in J Bradshaw and R Sainsbury (eds) *Experiencing Poverty*, Ashgate Publishing, Burlington, VT, 2000, pp. 268–88; E Trzcinski, 'Middle School Children's Perceptions on Welfare and Poverty: An Exploratory, Qualitative Study', *Journal of Family and Economic Issues*, 23:4, 2002, pp. 339–59.

[10] A Crowley and C Vulliamy, *Listen Up! Children and young people talk about poverty*, 2007. http://www.savethechildren.org.uk/en/docs/wales_lu_pov.pdf (Accessed October 2007.)

[11] See note 2.

[12] S E G Lea, A J Mewse and W Wrapson, *Understanding Debtor Behaviour* (in preparation); S E G Lea, P Webley and R M Levine, 'The economic psychology of consumer debt', *Journal of Economic Psychology*, 14 (1993), pp. 85–119.

[13] S E G Lea, A J Mewse and W Wrapson, *Understanding Debtor Behaviour* (in preparation); S E G Lea, P Webley and C M Walker, 'Psychological factors in consumer debt: Money management, economic socialization, and credit use', *Journal of Economic Psychology*, 16 (1995), pp. 681–701.

[14] R Ranyard and G Craig, 'Estimating the duration of a flexible loan: The effect of supplementary information', *Journal of Economic Psychology* 14 (1993), pp. 317–335; R Ranyard and G Craig, 'Evaluating and budgeting with instalment credit: An interview study', *Journal of Economic Psychology*, 16 (1995), pp. 449–67.

[15] T Kochuyt, 'Giving away one's poverty: on the consumption of scarce resources within the family' *Sociological Review*, 52:2 (2004), pp.139–61, and note 2 above.

[16] See S Payne, *Poverty, Social Exclusion and Mental Health: Findings from the 1999 PSE Survey*, Working Paper no. 15, Townsend Centre for International Poverty Research, University of Bristol, 1999.

[17] G Palmer, T MacInnes and P Kenway, *Monitoring poverty and social exclusion 2006*, Joseph Rowntree Foundation, York, 2006.

[18] M Byrne, E Agerbo, W W Eaton and P B Mortensen, 'Parental socio-economic status and risk of first admission with schizophrenia – A Danish national register based study', *Social Psychiatry and Psychiatric Epidemiology*, 39:2 (2004), pp. 87–96.

[19] For example, P R Amato and J Zuo, 'Rural poverty, urban poverty, and psychological well-being', *Sociological Quarterly*, 33 (1992), pp. 229–40.

[20] D Roker and J Coleman, '"The invisible poor": young people growing up in family poverty', in J Bradshaw and R Sainsbury (eds) *Experiencing poverty*, Ashgate Publishing, Burlington, VT, 2000.

[21] S E G Lea, A J Mewse and W Wrapson, *Understanding Debtor Behaviour* (in preparation).

[22] See note 21.

[23] See note 20.

[24] S M Hill, S Augustyniak, G J Duncan, G Gurin, P Gurin, J K Liker *et al*, *Motivation and Economic Mobility*, Institute for Social Research, University of Michigan, Ann Arbor, 1985.

[25] T J Kane, 'Giving back control: Long term poverty and motivation', *Social Service Review*, 61:3 (1987), pp. 405–19.

[26] L Lein, A F Benjamin, M McManus and K Roy, 'Economic roulette: when is a job not a job?', *Community Work and Family*, 8:4 (2005), pp. 359–78.

[27] See note 21.

[28] For example, P Taylor, C Funk and P Craighill, *Are We Happy Yet?*, Pew Research Center, Washington, DC, 2006.

[29] R W Belk, 'Three scales to measure constructs related to materialism: Reliability, validity, and relationships to measures of happiness', *Advances in Consumer Research*, 11 (1984), pp. 291–97.

[30] See, for example, N Garmezy, 'Resiliency and vulnerability to adverse developmental outcomes associated with poverty', *American Behavioral Scientist*, 34 (1991), pp. 416–30.

10 Stigma, shame and sense of worth

Matt Davies

> *"One of the most dreadful aspects of living in poverty is that everyone has an opinion about how you should live, regardless of the resources you have, and you are far more likely to come to the attention of the authorities in one form or another. Needing to ask for help is painful enough, but to be treated with disdain and distrust by those to whom you have to turn is a raw and humiliating experience."*[1]

The quote above exemplifies the experiences of families facing long-term poverty. This chapter is based on the work of ATD Fourth World[2] in working with some of the poorest and most disadvantaged families.

How parents define poverty

As part of a project to involve parents with experience of poverty in the training of social workers, participants were asked to define poverty:[3]

- being on the margins
- lack of power over your own life and a lack of choices
- having no voice; not being heard
- having no right to refuse services that you feel are inappropriate
- feeling inadequate
- having low self-esteem
- lack of status
- feeling shame and stigma
- not having enough money or support
- having a wealth of expertise in survival, courage and humility, but this not being recognised
- being blamed and judged by others for the situation you are in.

Living on benefits or low income – cause of shame and stigma

Many families experiencing long-term poverty are dependent on state benefits. Many of these families report that the perception of them in the media as 'scroungers' increases their sense of shame. One mother, when preparing an intervention at the All Party Parliamentary Group on Poverty, reported: "When you go down to the benefits office you've got to leave your dignity in your back pocket just to get what you're entitled to."[4]

This sense of stigma can be perpetuated by policy-makers and politicians using language such as 'high-cost, high-harm families' and 'adults with chaotic lifestyles'. We see plenty of campaigns telling us 'No Ifs, No Buts, Benefit Fraud is a Crime', but how often do we see similar campaigns about wealthy tax evaders defrauding us as a society? As a consequence, people living in poverty often feel they are to blame for the circumstances in which they find themselves.

But it is not only those on benefits who live in poverty, nor only they who wear the label of shame in their struggle to get by. A research project being carried out by ATD Fourth World, training peer researchers to carry out interviews with counterparts living in poverty, has found that even when working long hours, income for many remains low and barely enough to survive on, leading people to employ different measures to make money stretch.[5]

The consequences of this are numerous in terms of family life, including a lack of choice in terms of purchasing basic essentials of food, clothing, household goods and so on. But one of the most drastic consequences is the sense of isolation and exclusion associated with poverty, exacerbated by a sense of stigma and shame. In the research mentioned above, respondents reported an overwhelming sense of isolation, the lack of money preventing any opportunity for social life. One of the peer researchers from the project backed this up from her own experience: "The challenge for me is the isolation, the loneliness, the painful awareness that we are not able to join in society or play any part in it. We are spectators as we watch other people live, then struggle to survive to make a life for our children."[6]

This is also true for new arrivals in the country who have left behind a traditionally strong family support network, compounding their sense of isolation: "I find it very difficult to be a mum on my own. In my country you are never on your own, you have your mum around, your aunties, your friends. It is very tiring to be always on your own – and boring… you don't have anyone to discuss with, it is always you thinking about everything."[7]

People often have insufficient money to go for a drink or to the cinema with friends, and are ashamed of inviting friends to a flat with furnishings in a poor state of repair. As one member of ATD Fourth World reported in a recent conference at the TUC: "It's frightening to let anyone come in and see a home that has relied on the choices of charity and other people's décor."[8]

Role of services in perpetuating stigma and shame

Families living in poverty often experience enormous difficulties in accessing services, despite their right to use these services. They also face discrimination in the form of judgements from other people based on stereotypes of people living in poverty – or 'poverty-ism'.[9] Prejudices and preconceived ideas mean people experiencing poverty are at a disadvantage. An image of the 'poor person' is created without any personal knowledge of them: 'If you are on benefits you should have enough to get by; if you can't, you must waste your money on alcohol and cigarettes or spend it irresponsibly.' The stereotype can lead to suggestions that if you live in poverty you are likely to neglect your family.

Families report that insufficient account is taken of their material circumstances, and that there is a lack of understanding of how poverty affects their confidence to take up services potentially of benefit to them. Work by ATD Fourth World[10] on piloting a tool to reach the most disadvantaged families found that the limited take-up of services seemed to be due to service users:
- finding the attitudes of the professional staff in the services patronising
- thinking that services are not relevant to their needs
- being ashamed of being in need or fearful of being judged as unable to cope
- being worried about possible interference in their lives, about their control being undermined, or about their privacy being invaded
- being fully preoccupied and overwhelmed by their difficulties and not having the peace of mind to look for sources of support.

Many disadvantaged families live with the fear of their children being taken into care because of the intervention of local authority social services. This is backed up by recent research which showed that, for families in poverty, encounters with public services were perceived to be associated with the risk of losing resources, being misunderstood or harshly judged or, ultimately, losing their children.[11]

This makes families experiencing poverty reluctant to use any form of services. As one mother told ATD Fourth World, "When you're living in poverty, you don't answer the knock at the door. It's never good news: it's either the debt collector, the housing officer, the police or the social worker."

Role of policy-makers and service-providers in preventing shame and stigma

"People who live in poverty know the solutions to their problems better than anyone else. Asking their opinions and giving them a voice is essential if we are to come to any true understanding of poverty and what can be done to eradicate it." (Service-user participant in training programme)[12]

There are steps that can be taken to break down the sense of stigma, shame and lack of self-worth associated with poverty that prevent those who experience them from participating fully in society. However, it should be recognised that when fears are so entrenched, as outlined above, this will take time as well as considerable effort and resources.

One way to achieve this is to involve people with experience of poverty in the front-line training of relevant practitioners. As part of ATD Fourth World's work in building a training programme to increase the awareness of poverty among social workers, the following outcomes were drawn up:[13]

- **Self-awareness and poverty-awareness:** Have an understanding of service users' definitions of poverty; develop awareness of 'poverty-ism' (where people are discriminated against because of their poverty), of what families need in order to cope, and an understanding of what is 'good enough' in a family's circumstances; don't aim for something impossible.
- **Power and powerlessness:** Have an understanding of the fear and stress (and the potential effects of this on behaviour) that come with powerlessness in the face of local government institutions, and the fear that children could be removed; gain more knowledge about the difficulties of

inequality – the difference between rich and poor; develop awareness of societal double standards where 'multiple carers' aren't acceptable but 'au pairs' are OK.

- **Practical skills:** Provide training around recording – notes and report-writing – in a way that does not oppress families and individuals; have an understanding of the importance of service-user ownership of assessments; learn to distinguish risks that parents themselves create from needs that are created by a family's poverty; have an understanding of the need for statutory services to provide the financial wherewithal for people to make changes – eg, a suggested special diet for a child may be difficult on a family's current income.

- **A rights-based perspective:** Develop an understanding of the importance of independent advocacy for a family; have the ability to see the resilience of families and the positive qualities, skills and strengths that they show; practise not judging by appearances; have a deepened awareness of adults' rights as parents as well as children's rights; develop an understanding of social workers' own right to good supervision and support.

There is also a need to re-examine the methodology used by service-providers and policy-makers in reaching the most disadvantaged. This is particularly relevant given the current aims of the government to target intervention on the "most excluded 2% of families who have not been lifted by the rising tide of living standards and increased opportunity, and who remain in poverty with complex needs, multiple problems and low aspiration".[14]

Over the course of 18 months, ATD Fourth World worked with a Sure Start local programme to pilot a project in order to develop an outreach tool to reach the most disadvantaged families. The following lessons emerged, which are transferable to all kinds of service provision:[15]

- To be effective, outreach tools need to combine a proactive approach with a willingness to adapt to how people feel from week to week. Families should not be expected to fit in with a model the service-provider has decided on in advance.

- To be effective, outreach tools and services should review their routine administrative processes, particularly those elements that make the services threatening for vulnerable families. Think twice: do people really need to give their name and address when they first use a service or to sign in when they arrive?

- Families should not have to justify their need for services. To be effective, outreach tools and services should not start by asking families about their problems. People should be free to share what they want of their lives, when they feel ready.
- To be effective, outreach tools, services and – above all – their funders must be prepared to make a long-term commitment. They must recognise and accept that they may not be able to show concrete evidence of success within a few months.
- To be effective, outreach tools must give priority to those who are most affected by poverty and social exclusion, rather than aiming for the highest numbers.
- To be effective, outreach tools and services need to address what a family wants – not just provide what providers think a family needs. Services must be prepared to be shaped by what families ask for.
- To be effective, outreach tools must find the means to involve the whole community.

Conclusion

Clearly, the stigma associated with poverty is a difficult barrier to overcome, for those directly affected, and for practitioners and services attempting to reach them. Nevertheless, this should not prevent people experiencing poverty from being treated equally, especially when attempting to receive that to which they are entitled.

Policy-makers and practitioners at all levels can contribute to breaking down the feelings of shame and consequent isolation. As one grass-roots member of ATD Fourth World writes:

> *"Poor parents, does not equal poor parenting. Families living in poverty do not want pity or sympathy, nor do they want the label of lazy scroungers or criminals. They want to be able to be a part of society, contribute to it and have their abilities and resilience recognised. Most of all, they want to be empowered, not forced, to help themselves out of poverty."* [16]

Notes

[1] M Roberts, 'Estate Life', *N16 Magazine*, 30 (2006).

[2] ATD Fourth World is a voluntary organisation working alongside people experiencing long-term poverty. Member of the International Movement ATD Fourth World, a non-governmental organisation (NGO) with general consultative status with the Economic and Social Council (ECOSOC) of the United Nations, it has been forming partnerships with very poor families in order to combat poverty in the UK for more than 40 years. More information on its UK work can be found at www.atd-uk.org

[3] ATD Fourth World, *"Getting the Right Trainers": Enabling service users to train social work students and practitioners about the realities of family poverty in the UK*, 2005.

[4] Quote taken from an ATD Fourth World policy forum to prepare an intervention at the All Party Parliamentary Group on Poverty in 2004.

[5] Taken from initial findings from a forthcoming research report, *Voices for a Change*, to be published in 2008.

[6] Taken from minutes of a meeting to prepare *Voices for a Change* (see note 5).

[7] ATD Fourth World, *"Not Too Hard to Reach": Developing a tool to reach the most disadvantaged families*, 2006.

[8] K Kelly, speech given at TUC Poverty Conference, 17 October 2007.

[9] ATD Fourth World, 2005 (see note 3).

[10] ATD Fourth World, 2006 (see note 7).

[11] K Canvin, C Jones, A Martitla, B Burström and M Whitehead, '"Can I risk using public services?" Perceived consequences of seeking help and health care among households in poverty: qualitative study', *Journal of Epidemiology and Community Health*, 61 (2007), pp. 984–89.

[12] ATD Fourth World, 2005 (see note 3).

[13] ATD Fourth World, *"Getting the Right Trainers": Enabling service users to train social work students and practitioners about the realities of family poverty in the UK*, 2005.

[14] Cabinet Office, *Reaching Out: Think families*, The Stationery Office, London, 2007.

[15] ATD Fourth World, 2006 (see note 7).

[16] A Dyer, 'Poor but still proud', *Parliamentary Brief*, August 2006.

11 Time and money

David Piachaud

"Getting and spending we lay waste our hours"
(after W B Yeats)

Introduction

Money and time are closely linked. Mephistopheles offered Dr Faustus all the delights of the world for 20 years, in exchange for his soul. Similar, if not quite so dramatic, choices face many people. Time cannot be directly bought or sold; what can of course be bought is the use of other people's time and one's own time can be sold – indeed, most of economics is concerned with this market economy. The combination of constraints and circumstances mean that the choices people have in earning and consuming – in getting and spending – are very different, and highly unequal. It is these inequalities that are explored here.

Getting

It is a truism that the money you get, in terms of the hourly rate of pay, determines the hours of work required to reach any given level of gross earnings. To reach, say, £300 earnings (about two-thirds of average earnings) requires 54 hours at the national minimum wage but only 26 hours at the average wage rate. Working out the hours of work at the minimum wage (NMW) needed to reach the government's own poverty level (of 60% of median income level) is not, however, as simple as it sounds. First, the poverty level varies with household size. Second, net income depends not only on earning but on deductions for income tax and national insurance contributions and additions from tax credits and child benefit. Third, there may be more than one earner, which affects tax liability. Assuming there is only one earner, the poverty levels and the hours required to reach these for different households were in April 2007 as follows:

Table 1: Hours of work at national minimum wage (NMW) to reach poverty level, April 2007

	Poverty level (1)	Gross earnings to reach poverty level at NMW (2)	Hours of paid work to reach poverty level at NMW (3)
Single person, aged 25 or over	£129 pw	£230 pw	43
Couple, no children	£192 pw	£332 pw	62
Couple, 1 child (aged 8)	£230 pw	£297 pw	56
Couple, 2 children (aged 8, 10)	£269 pw	£304 pw	57
Couple, 3 children (aged 6, 8, 10)	£332 pw	£357 pw	67

Notes and sources:

1. Poverty levels are 60% of median equivalised disposable income after housing costs (Department of Work and Pensions [DWP], Households Below Average Income (HBAI) 1994/95–2005/06, The Stationery Office, London, 2007). These are updated to April 2007 based on rise in household gross disposable income per head (Office for National Statistics, *UK Economic Accounts*, ONS Online, October 2007, Table 1.06).
2. Gross earnings are from DWP, *Tax Benefit Model Tables, April 2007*, 2007.
3. Hours = gross earnings/national minimum wage (£5.35 per hour in April 2007).

To reach the poverty level being paid at the minimum wage requires hours far above average working time. The money you get determines the time you must work to make ends meet.

Rising wage inequalities have been matched by a higher dispersion of the distribution of working hours, with, in particular, those at the very bottom and those at the top of the wage distribution working longer hours. While those at the top of the wage distribution work longer because of the high rewards, low earners have to work longer hours simply to reach the poverty level.

Many of the low paid have to take second jobs to boost their income. Of those aged over 21, 2.7% of men and 5.1% of women had second jobs; the hourly wage in second jobs were, for most, lower than in first job or only jobs.[1] For some, particularly lone parents, gaining a meagre income requires an exhausting combination of two or more jobs, unsocial hours often very late at night or very early in the morning, travel without a car, and on top of that all the demands of childcare.

The true time costs of work depend on the hours worked and on when they are worked. Working at 4pm is very different from working at 4am, just as playing with a baby at 4pm is very different from 'playing' at 4am. It is therefore relevant to consider reliance on unsocial hours and on multiple jobs. Exploring these aspects also reveals how time involves "important coordination problems",[2] as the time available for care or other activities is affected not only by the total amount of hours of paid employment, but by how these hours are distributed.

A study conducted in 2001 found that 21% of mothers and 41% of fathers worked early mornings (6.00–8.30am), 14% of mothers and 17% of fathers worked evenings or nights (after 8.30pm) and 18% of mothers and 22% of fathers worked every Saturday and on Sunday at least once a month.[3] Parents in lower socio-economic groups were more likely than those in professional jobs to feel they had no option but to work at atypical times.

More recent research showed that many more parents are now at work when their children are at home.[4] If unsocial hours are defined as any work done outside 8am to 7pm, Monday to Friday, around 80% of working fathers and more than half of working mothers work some unsocial hours. In two-fifths of all families at least one parent is working regularly at weekends; more than a quarter of working lone parents work at weekends. Working unsocial hours inevitably reduces the time parents spend with their children: for example, fathers in sole-earner families who work at unsocial times spent on average 10.5 hours per week less with their children than those not working unsocial hours. Similarly, in dual-earner families mothers who work at unsocial times spend eight hours less with their children.

The times at which men and women worked were investigated by Susan Harkness for the Equal Opportunities Commission.[5] In the 1970s night work was primarily carried out by men in the manufacturing sector. Now it increasingly involves women in the service sector. The proportions working evening and nights in 2000 are shown in Table 2.

Table 2: Evening and night work by sex

	Men	Women
Proportion working: Evenings Nights	20% 17%	20% 9%
Proportion working nights: With degree With no qualifications	8% 20%	6% 9%

Source: S Harkness, *Low Pay, Time of Work and Gender,* Equal Opportunities Commission, London, 2002.

While some city lawyers and accountants may occasionally work through the night (in exchange for bonuses beyond the dreams of avarice), Harkness found that in general, night work is more prevalent among those with no qualifications, as shown in Table 2. Whereas men usually received a wage premium for working in the evening or at night, women generally did not do so. Thus low-skilled men could use unsocial hours to avoid low pay, but women could not do so.

Domestic obligations are rarely mentioned in economics textbooks but the reality for most people is that their lives are constrained, and this is especially true for parents with children and individuals caring for relatives with disabilities or those with disabilities themselves. In these situations there are not 24 hours to be allocated between paid work and leisure. Rather, the first requirement is to care for children, for the disabled person or for themselves. In part, that care may consist of time spent working on household tasks for no financial reward; in part it may involve being present, available if needed, yet unavailable for work outside the home. A study into time spent caring for very young children found that, on average, childcare tasks took just over seven hours per day.[6]

Time constraints determine whether people can enter the labour market and the hours they can work. Nearly half of women in paid work were working under 30 hours per week. They suffered a part-time wage penalty, as shorter working hours receive much lower hourly pay than full-time jobs.[7]

In short, the possibility of earning money – of 'getting' – is limited by time constraints, yet those with the lowest hourly pay need the most time in paid work to get enough to live on.

Spending

Time-saving goods

In some respects the home has become the locus of more activities. Gershuny looked at the changing consumption patterns of British households between 1959 and 1977 and concluded that there was a "process of substitution… taking place – of domestic machinery for domestic services, of motor cars for purchased transport services, of televisions and stereo systems for cinema".[8]

Whereas it is complicated to establish how much domestic appliances affect time spent on housework, it is clear that *not possessing* some devices results in certain tasks taking more time and more money. Take, for example, the task of washing clothes: 95% of households in Britain owned a washing machine in 2005/06, compared with 65% in 1970.[9] Thus, washing machines are now almost universal in Britain. Yet 350,000 elderly people living on their own and 50,000 lone parents do not have a washing machine. For them, to wash their clothes, sheets and towels often involves a trip to a launderette that may in terms of time – getting there, washing and drying – take one-and-a-half hours, and cost at least £2. Owning a washing machine saves time and money; those who cannot afford the capital cost or lack the space to have one face a substantial time cost.

A car is probably the most time-saving possession. Three-quarters of all households in Britain have a car (or more than one). Yet 10% of couples with children, 45% of lone parents, and three-fifths of elderly people living on their own have *not* have a car.[10] It is those without cars who now bear the greatest time burden – although whether the whole society benefits from the levels of congestion and pollution created by car ownership is more doubtful.

Half a century ago most regular shopping was done by walking to local shops and carrying the shopping home. Without fridges or freezers and limited by what could be carried, this involved shopping trips almost every day, largely undertaken by women. Now the bulk of shopping for most households involves one weekly trip by car to a supermarket. Not only are supermarkets substantially cheaper than local, corner shops,[11] but a large amount of time is saved – which is clearly why the share of the shopping in supermarkets has steadily increased. Consider, then, the relative position of those without a car who cannot carry large loads, because they are elderly or have small children in tow, who cannot travel far without the expense and delays of public transport, and who are restricted to the dwindling number of local shops with their high prices (as turnover declines, they have to increase their mark-up to make a living). The car-less lose out heavily in terms of time and money and this is exacerbated by poor public transport, especially in rural areas.

Put simply, those who can afford time-saving equipment save time. Those worst-off cannot do so.

Time-saving services

Barbara Ehrenreich, a leading journalist, investigated the challenge of living on low paid jobs in the USA[12] – a study that inspired Polly Toynbee's *Hard Work*.[13] After she finished her "gruelling, hair raising and darkly funny odyssey" she returned to her "customary place in the socio-economic spectrum". She wrote: "To go from the bottom 20 percent to the top 20 percent is to enter a magical world where needs are met, problems are solved, almost without any intermediate effort. If you want to get somewhere fast, you hail a cab… If you are part of the upper-middle class that employs a maid or maid service, you return from work to find the house miraculously restored to order – the toilet bowls shit-free and gleaming, the socks that you left on the floor levitated back to their normal dwelling place… Hundreds of little things get done, reliably and routinely every day, without anyone seeming to do them."[14]

Just as cleaning can be purchased from others whose hourly rate is usually much lower, many other service tasks that were traditionally performed in the home can now be 'outsourced'. Very few can now afford a cook; the millions 'in service' who served the rich and the middle classes one hundred years ago are long gone. But the time spent on preparing food, for example, can be reduced in many ways: one can go to a restaurant, have food delivered at home, buy take-away food from the shop, or warm up prepared food bought at the supermarket. Britain is experiencing an industrialisation of food preparation that has major effects on time use, on gender equality, on family life and on nutrition. It is one example of how having more money to buy services can save time, although it does not necessarily end up with any improvement in wellbeing.

Gershuny sees a process of convergence taking place, with women taking on more paid work and men taking on more unpaid work.[15] Yet while there may be a degree of convergence on average, Gershuny largely ignores inequalities in time burdens that reflect and reinforce poverty. It is those most constrained by poverty who are least able to buy services to save time.

Leisure time

Gershuny's studies of the use of time led him to conclude that most countries have experienced an increase in leisure time and that class differences have diminished, with the rich working more and the poor having more leisure. Yet differences remain huge and most mothers are time-poor and most low-paid workers, predominantly women, are either money-poor or time-poor or both.

Affluence has always been denoted by the availability of leisure time. The 'idle rich' were contrasted with the working classes. Leisure time is still very unequally distributed. As discussed above, the longest working hours are worked by those at either end of the earnings ladder; both those at the bottom and those at the top of the earning ladder work long hours. Yet there is no limit to the money that can be spent during leisure time and those at the top can buy 'luxury leisure'. Health spas, skiing, luxury hotels, all-inclusive packages – all symbolise the possibility of expensive enjoyment of leisure time. In short, it seems that the *way* in which leisure time is spent is becoming more important in determining social differentiation and inequality.

The impact of unsocial hours has been discussed in relation to family responsibilities and unequal pay, but it also has repercussions on leisure time and ways in which it can be enjoyed. As most social activities take place in the evening and during the weekend, those who work these hours are automatically excluded. The longed-for leisure time of many working poor families is interrupted by paid work and unpaid housework tasks.

Conclusion

Lack of money means lack of material resources. For most on low incomes it also means a lack of time. This is because a low rate of pay means long hours of work are needed to gain a poverty level income, because those caring for children and those with disabilities spend long hours on unpaid work, and because a low income means there is less possibility of saving time by buying time-saving goods and services.

There is now growing concern at the extent of time-poverty in modern life; this may be felt at all income levels. For the prosperous – rushing from country home to town, between holidays and work, downloading photos and uploading music, getting the central-locking system repaired and the broken DVD remote control replaced – such time-poverty is a regrettable reflection of lifestyle choices. For those who suffer both financial poverty and time poverty, the lack of time is a constant reminder of why money matters.

Notes

[1] H Robinson and J Wadsworth, *Did the Minimum Wage Affect the Incidence of Second Job Holding in Britain?*, Research Report for the Low Pay Commission, London, 2004.

[2] N Folbre, 'A theory of the misallocation of time', in N Folbre and M Bittman (eds) *Family time: the social organization of care*, Routledge, London, 2004.

[3] I La Valle, S Arthur, C Millward and J Scott, *Happy Families? Atypical work and its influence on family life*, Policy Press, Bristol, 2002.

[4] Relationship Foundation, All Work and No Pay?, London, 2006. http://www.relationshipsfoundation.org/download.php?id=147

[5] S Harkness, *Low Pay, Time of Work and Gender*, EOC Research Discussion series and Working Paper series, Equal Opportunities Commission, London, 2002.

[6] D Piachaud, *Round about Fifty Hours a Week: The time costs of children*, Child Poverty Action Group, London, 1984.

[7] A Manning and B Petrongolo, *The Part-time Pay Penalty*, CEP Discussion Paper no. 679, Centre for Economic Performance, London, 2005.

[8] J Gershuny, *Social Innovation and the Division of Labour*, Oxford University Press, Oxford, 1983.

[9] Office for National Statistics (ONS), *Family Spending: 2006 edition*, The Stationery Office, London, 2007, Table A51.

[10] ONS, 2007, Table A52 (see note 9).

[11] D Piachaud and J Webb, *The Price of Food*, STICERD, London, 1996.

[12] B Ehrenreich, *Nickel and Dimed*, Granta, London, 2002.

[13] P Toynbee, *Hard Work*, Bloomsbury, London, 2003.

[14] Ehrenreich, 2002, p.215 (see note 12).

[15] J Gershuny, *Changing Times: Work and leisure in postindustrial society*, Oxford University Press, New York, 2000.

Part 3

Ensuring a decent income for all

12 The cost of necessities

Jonathan Bradshaw

Introduction

Necessities are things people need. But need for what – to survive physically? Or to "satisfy prevailing standards of what is necessary for health, efficiency, the nurture of children and for participation in community activities"?[1] Or "one that affords full opportunity to participate in contemporary society and the basic options it offers. It is moderate in the sense of lying above the requirements of survival and decency, and well below levels of luxury as generally understood"?[2]

When Seebohm Rowntree undertook his first survey of poverty in York in 1898,[3] he used a budget standard. "In order to arrive at a minimum sum necessary to maintain families of various sizes in a state of physical efficiency", he priced a basket of food that would deliver a certain level of calorific intake for men, women and children. He added to this an allowance for clothing and fuel based on (rather casual) enquiries of what working-class families actually spent. He revised his budget standards in his subsequent studies in the light of new knowledge about nutritional science and he added items that perhaps had less to do with physical efficiency.

The budget standard that he had developed for his 1936 study of poverty in York helped to inform Beveridge's recommendations for the 'minimum subsistence' scale rates of benefits that were implemented in the post-war period. The benefit rates we have today therefore have their origins in conceptions of minimum necessities and minimum subsistence.

Uprating benefit rates

Of course benefit rates in real terms are considerably higher than they were when first introduced.[4] From 1948 until the mid-1970s there was no formal uprating policy. However, benefits were uprated, first in an ad hoc way, and then annually at least in line with movements in the Retail Price Index (RPI). In fact most benefits doubled their value in real terms and maintained their value in relation to average earnings. The Conservative government in 1973 decided to distinguish between 'long-term' and 'short-term' benefits. Labour, in 1977, began to link long-term benefits to movements in earnings or prices, whichever was higher, and short-term benefits were to be linked at least to prices. This arrangement did not last long because the Conservative government first abandoned the link with earnings and then adapted price indexation by introducing in 1982 the Rossi index (supplementary benefit [SB] and associated means-tested benefit were to be uprated by the RPI less housing costs) on the grounds that people on SB had their housing costs covered by the state.

As a result, a gap began to emerge between the net income of people in employment and people on benefits, and between those people receiving benefits that were uprated by at least movements in the RPI, and those receiving benefits, which were uprated by the Rossi index. However, none of this was formalised in legislation and nor was any principle adhered to consistently: some benefits – including child benefit – were not uprated at all in a number of years.

When the Labour government came to power in 1997, it inherited this system and eventually in some ways adopted it more formally than its predecessors. Although there are no more legislative requirements to uprate benefits than there were a decade ago, the current government has been more ready to announce uprating *policies* for specific benefits. There have also been substantial improvements in the real levels of some benefits, usually in favour of children and pensioners.

When setting benefit levels and their differentials, a government has to have regard to the resources available, the relative needs of different types of claimant, how their labour supply, savings, family formation and other behaviour might be influenced by financial incentives, and no doubt the political costs and benefits of their decisions. However, the present situation is absurd – partly as a result of uprating policy. From April 2008:

* A single pregnant woman 18–24 gets £47.95 per week on income support (IS).
* A single unemployed woman aged 59 gets £60.50 per week on IS.

- When she is 60 she will have her income raised by pension credit to at least £124.05.
- The basic retirement pension for a single person is only £90.70.
- A lone parent with one child on IS gets £60.50 for herself and £64.70 for the child.

All this has completely disrupted the implied equivalence structure in the scales of benefits – which were anyway never based on a very secure foundation!

There is no rationale for the differentials in the level of benefits. There is no basis in need, justice or equity; no basis in concerns about incentives; and if the uprating of benefits of single and childless couples by Rossi and other price indices continues, it is going to generate a huge increase in poverty and general detachment from society for large numbers of long-term unemployed people (including many suffering with mental illness).

Poverty research

Running in parallel with the benefit uprating story has been academic and government poverty research. In the post-war period the conceptualisation (and operationalisation) of poverty has been influenced more by the thinking of Townsend than by Rowntree. Townsend provided an intellectual framework that enables us to think about poverty in developing and developed countries, and over time, through his concept of relative deprivation. Poverty was not merely the inability to purchase necessities for a minimum subsistence, it was about those who:

> "… lack resources to obtain the types of diet, participate in the activities and have the living conditions and amenities which are customary, or at least widely encouraged or approved, in the societies to which they belong. Their resources are so seriously below those commanded by the average individual or family that they are in effect excluded from ordinary living patterns, customs and activities." [5]

A variety of methods have been used to operationalise this conception. Townsend himself used social indicators and the 'Breadline Britain' studies[6, 7, 8] developed the methodology into socially perceived necessities. Government poverty measures started with a threshold based on benefit rates plus a margin, in the *Low Income Statistics* series. Then this was dropped in favour of a degree of inequality measure in the *Household Below Average Income* series, which adopted a threshold of equivalent income less than 60% of the median. Now the child poverty targets are being monitored by a relative measure fixed in time, the contemporary relative measure and an indicator that combines income poverty with a deprivation of items and activities. Poverty has also been measured using subjective measures, consumption data and, once again, budget standards.

Modern budget standards

It was partly in response to the chaos in both uprating policy, and poverty measurement methods, that budget standards were reinvented[9] in the post-war period.[10] The Family Budget Unit (FBU) at the University of York sought to develop a method for establishing adequacy (see Chapter 13), or at least to enable debate to take place about whether people on benefits could afford necessities. It was hoped that a budget standard poverty threshold might resonate better with the general public than relative income measures.

Initially, in a project funded by the Joseph Rowntree Foundation, the FBU drew up budget standards for a limited set of family types at a "modest but adequate level". This budget was then adapted to represent a "low-cost budget but adequate", which at the time was considerably higher than the level of income support for families with children and pensioners. When the report on the research was published the following exchange took place in the House of Commons:

> *"**Mr Donald Dewar** (Labour Spokesman): 'The report underlined the difficulties in making ends meet at current income support levels. Does the right hon. Gentleman accept that there is little room for comfort when – according to the report's findings – a couple with two children under 11, living in a council house, need an extra £36 per week to fund the austere low-cost budget? There are no signs that this Minister and this Government have any visible active commitment to tackling problems of poverty.'*

> *"**Mr Peter Lilley** (Secretary of State for Social Security): 'The hon. Gentleman said that the Rowntree report spelt out an "austere low-costs budget", a budget that allows the poorest only a video recorder, a camera and a television set; … '"*
>
> (*Hansard* cols 1018 and 1020, 12 November 1992)

The FBU's budget standards had not succeeded in establishing agreement about what constituted necessities. However, it could be said that there was the start of a debate about what items and activities people should be able to afford.

Following the initial research project the FBU published a succession of budgets (see http://www.york.ac.uk/res/fbu/publications.htm). There were moments of success. There were substantial real increases in in-work and out-of-work benefits for children in 2000. In 2001, after Age Concern published an FBU pensioner budget,[11] there was a substantial increase in minimum income guarantee to exactly match the recommended budget standard. The publication of the single person's budget may have helped to draw attention to living standards of young single pregnant women on IS and influence the introduction of the Sure Start maternity grant, the extension of child benefit to pregnant women, and now the 'health in pregnancy' grant. Budget standards have been increasingly used in the courts to inform decisions about the affordability of fines; by financial advisory agencies; in setting the level of foster care allowances; and in personal compensation cases over the costs of injuries to a child. Others have since produced excellent budgets, including Middleton[12,13] and Smith *et al*,[14] Age Concern,[15] Saunders[16] in Australia and the Vincentian Partnership in Ireland.[17]

Associated with the work on budget standards is the FBU's exploration of expenditure data[18,19] in order to establish the costs of necessities. As an example of the approach, Figure 1 uses five years of the Expenditure and Food Survey 2001–2005 uprated by movements in the commodity RPI to February 2007. Expenditure on necessities for this purpose is defined as expenditure on food, fuel and clothing. Expenditure has been plotted for each decile group of total expenditure (less housing costs). It can be seen that necessity expenditure for this family type varies from an average of about £88 per week for the bottom decile to £230 per week for the top decile. Necessities take 41% of all expenditure of the bottom decile, compared with 17% for the top decile. Marked on Figure 1 (overleaf) are the points on the distribution where the average expenditure of families with two children on IS are located – right at the bottom: they are spending £95 per week or 42% of their total expenditure on these commodities.

This kind of expenditure analysis could be the basis for establishing the costs necessities. If households have to spend more than 10% of their income on

Figure 1: Expenditure on necessities: couple plus two children

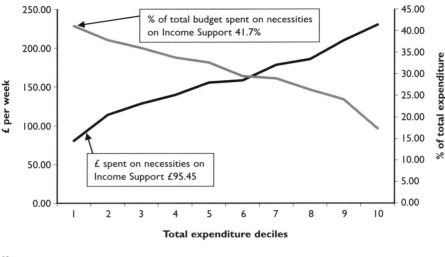

Key
— £
— % of total

fuel, they are officially classed as living in fuel poverty. The original Orshansky US poverty measure was based on the income of households spending more than 30% of their incomes on food.

Developments in budget standards research

The FBU budgets had last been rebased to take account of rising living standards in 1989. After that they were uprated by movements in the commodity RPI. But as a result of benefit increases by the Labour government the FBU budgets had become out of date. The budget standards needed to be rebased.

With the support of the Joseph Rowntree Foundation the FBU is now engaged in that endeavour. The FBU budgets had been based on normative methods – basically, experts applied their minds to what families should have in order to meet a given living standard. Experts decided how long items should last and what the quality and price of items should be. They had regard to norms such as the nutritional adequacy of the diet. Published standards – space standards, thermal standards, alcoholic drink standards – were also consulted. The FBU drew on research on, for example, the lifetimes of clothing, white goods, consumption and shopping patterns. But in the end the budgets were normative. In contrast, Middleton and colleagues at the University of Loughborough had been developing budget standards based on qualitative empirical methods. Their budgets were informed by what focus groups representing different family types decided was necessary.

The Loughborough team and the FBU at York have joined forces to combine their respective budget methodologies to produce minimum income standards (MIS) for the UK. The results will be produced during 2008. Users will be able to go on to the project website, specify a family type, alter some of the assumptions for expenditure on variable items, and generate a transparent budget standard. This will, at the same time, estimate what the level of expenditure on each commodity should be, what net wage it takes to generate that budget, given the current tax benefit system, and how the budget compares with the out-of-work benefit rates. The project will make recommendations for a method of updating and rebasing the MIS. It is hoped that it will be used to generate evidence about necessities, the adequacy of benefit rates, and the equivalent needs of families of different sizes and composition.

Notes

[1] US Bureau of Labour Statistics City Worker's Family Budget, quoted in M Wynn, *Family Policy*, London: Michael Joseph, London, 1970, p.36.

[2] H Watts, *New American Budget Standards: Report of the Expert Committee on Family Budget Revision*, University of Wisconsin, Institute for Research on Poverty, 1980, p.viii.

[3] B S Rowntree, *Poverty: A study of town life*, Centennial ed., The Policy Press, Bristol, 2000 reprint.

[4] J Bradshaw and T Lynes, *Benefit Uprating Policy and Living Standards*, Social Policy Reports no. 1, Social Policy Research Unit, University of York, York, 1995.

[5] P Townsend, *Poverty in the United Kingdom*, Allen Lane, London, 1979, p. 31.

[6] J Mack and S Lansley, *Poor Britain*, London: Allen and Unwin, 1985.

[7] D Gordon and C Patazis, *Breadline Britain in the 1990s*, Ashgate: Aldershot, 1997.

[8] D Gordon, L Adelman, K Ashworth, J Bradshaw, R Levitas, S Middleton, C Pantazis, D Patsios, S Payne, P Townsend and J Williams, *Poverty and Social Exclusion in Britain*, Joseph Rowntree Foundation, York, 2000.

[9] J Bradshaw (ed) *Budget Standards for the United Kingdom*, Studies in Cash & Care, Avebury, Aldershot, 1994.

[10] For a history of budget standards research see G Fisher, *An Overview of Recent Work on Standard Budgets in the United States and Other Anglophone Countries*, 2007. http://aspe.hhs.gov/poverty/papers/std-budgets/

[11] H Parker (ed) *Low Cost but Acceptable Incomes for Older People: A minimum income standard for households aged 65–74 years in the UK*, Policy Press, Bristol, 2000.

[12] S Middleton, 'Agreeing Poverty Lines: The Development of Consensual Budget Standards Methodology', in J Bradshaw and J Sainsbury (eds) *Researching Poverty*, Ashgate, Aldershot, 2000, pp. 59–76.

[13] S Middleton, 'The adequacy of benefits for children', in G Preston (ed) *At Greatest Risk*, Child Poverty Action Group, London, 2005.

[14] N Smith, S Middleton, K Ashton-Brooks, L Cox and B Dobson with L Reith, *Disabled People's Costs of Living: More than you would think*, Joseph Rowntree Foundation, York, 2004.

[15] C Deeming, 'Minimum Income Standards: How might budget standards be set for the UK?', *Journal of Social Policy*, October; 34:4 (2005), pp. 1–18.

[16] P Saunders, *Using Budget Standards to Assess the Well-Being of Families*, Social Policy Research Centre Discussion Paper no. 93, Social Policy Research Centre, University of New South Wales, Sydney, NSW, Australia, 1998. http://www.sprc.unsw.edu.au/dp/dp093.pdf

[17] Vincentian Partnership for Social Justice, *Low Cost But Acceptable Budgets for Three Households*, Dublin, 2004.

[18] J R Bradshaw, D Mitchell and J Morgan, 'Evaluating adequacy: the potential of budget standards', *Journal of Social Policy*, 16:2 (1987), pp. 165–181.

[19] P Saunders, J Bradshaw and M Hirst, 'Using household expenditure to develop an income poverty line', *Social Policy and Administration*, 36:3 (2002), pp. 217–34.

13 How low-income families use their money

Fran Bennett

This chapter argues that research has shown that most parents living on a low income prioritise their children's needs above their own, and that this is particularly true of mothers, who tend to manage the household budget and be the main 'shock-absorbers' of poverty in low-income families.[1] It reviews more specific evidence regarding the impact of recent increases in income on the spending patterns of lower-income parents and on child wellbeing. Finally, it discusses the importance of looking at what goes on within the household, and debates the difficult issues of budgeting skills and whether increases in income are sufficient in themselves to transform the lives of children in low-income families.

Parents try to protect children from poverty

Children depend on their parents' decisions for how much they benefit from family income; and, as Gregg *et al* note, "when policy makers seek to raise income transfers for the support of children, there is a concern that the money may not be spent with the interests of the child in mind".[2] In fact, however, there is solid evidence that low-income parents try hard to protect their children from the effects of poverty.[3] So hard do they try that, according to one study, the amount spent on children tends not to vary much by family income level, meaning that disproportionate amounts are spent by those on lower incomes.[4] Only if parents' incomes are squeezed to the limit does this become impossible.[5]

Qualitative research with children themselves has demonstrated how they are not passive recipients of this parental self-sacrifice, however; children try hard to mediate the impact of poverty on their parents as well, especially to protect them from feelings of inadequacy and shame.[6] But this nuances, rather than negates, the overall picture of parents' prioritising of their children's needs.

There is also clear evidence that mothers are more likely to manage the household finances in low-income families, where money is tight;[7] and that they are particularly likely to put their family's needs and wants above their own.[8] This takes its toll on their own health and wellbeing,[9] though they may also be proud of their skills.[10]

Of course, as in all income groups, there are some who do not manage their money as well as others.[11] Drug or other substance dependence will undermine parents' efforts to protect their children. But many critics of low-income parents have no idea of the tenacity and determination needed just to keep going, in particular when these parents feel lacking in the resources to give their children a decent upbringing, and undervalued by the outside world.[12] And an overview of qualitative studies of low-income families stressed that most learn to budget better with experience, and "the evidence for fecklessness is scant".[13] They exercise control over their spending whenever possible, but (as the author points out) have little control over most factors that really make a difference to their lives.

Evidence on impact of increased incomes

As Jane Waldfogel has argued, "income and poverty measures capture the resources potentially available to children but are potentially flawed in that they do not measure the resources actually spent on children".[14] The overview cited above concluded that the injection of (even small) amounts of additional resources could lead to significant improvements in low-income families' lives. Recent research has highlighted the impact on lower-income families' spending patterns of the improvements in incomes under the Labour government, looking at 1996/97 (before it came to power) up to 2000/01.[15] The research focused on families with younger children, as they saw larger increases in benefits.[16] The method employed allowed the impact of the income rise to be isolated from other changes.

Low-income families (in the bottom third of the income distribution) seem to have spent the extra money in ways that resulted in their spending patterns becoming more like those of more affluent families, but with greater emphasis on clothing, household goods/services and transport and a reduced share of income going on housing, alcohol and tobacco. They increased their spending on food in real terms. As income rose, parents spent more on child-related goods (including children's clothing, toys and books), leading to spending converging with that of better-off families.[17]

As Gregg *et al* concluded, "There is, then, very striking evidence that low-income families are using their additional income in ways that are likely to benefit children" (p. 265). Parents also increased spending on their own clothing and footwear. Ownership of consumer durables became more equal, though this varied by item (with lower rates of computer ownership continuing).

A comparison of the impacts of welfare reforms in the USA and UK[18] notes that there is as yet no large-scale study in the UK that relates the impact of these reforms to child health and development outcomes. But the authors of the previous study suggest that low-income families should be experiencing less hardship and improved wellbeing, and that this is what other recent research in the UK has shown.

For example, analysis of the Families and Children Study (FACS) found significant increases in incomes (especially for working families and couples) between 1999 and 2001.[19] Material wellbeing had improved for families out of work as well as for those in work. The reduction in the proportion of children in the panel sample suffering severe or moderate hardship[20] led the authors, Vegeris and Perry, to argue that "families are using their extra finances to improve living conditions for their children" (p. 10); they highlighted improved nutrition, clothing and family entertainment. They concluded that policies leading to further rises in family incomes[21] would benefit children.

Qualitative research, also based on FACS, explored the impact of an increase in income in more depth.[22] Interviews were conducted in 2002 with 22 lone parents and 15 people in couples who had been involved in FACS in 2000 and 2001.[23] All had had a family member moving into employment. The key indicator for improved financial wellbeing was an increase in discretionary income (after essential outgoings); households with smaller increases saw only very small improvements in living standards – often limited to children.

Those who were better off in work spent the extra income on their priorities, which included housing, fuel, food and clothing; but, as the authors (Farrell and O'Connor) noted, "children consistently remained every household's main priority both prior to, and following, the move into work" (p. 4). Families' food improved in quantity and then quality, and treats were common, especially for children; houses were decorated or furnished, extended or purchased; and more clothing was bought. Children saw improvements before their parents did. However, parents bought branded clothing regardless of their financial wellbeing, to avoid their children being taunted; paradoxically, this shows the importance of the non-material side of poverty, and the powerful threat of labelling or 'othering' of children for signs of difference.[24]

Families also spent on holidays or daytrips, often for the first time. 'Luxuries' were also bought for children (and, in better-off households, for parents too). In general, children benefited most, with the parents benefiting indirectly; households had to be significantly better off before adults started to see a direct material benefit.[25] Psychological benefits for children included pleasure from material improvements; fitting in more with their peers; and less stress and arguing caused by money worries. But tensions included resentment at the time their parent(s) spent in employment.

Another study examined the impact of paid work in the longer term. In 2004 interviews were conducted with 29 families who had been involved in FACS in 2001 and in 2002, and who had a family member who had moved into employment.[26] Sustained work had generally led to improvements in financial and material circumstances. Families saw improvements in housing, food and clothing, and could start to buy luxuries. Children were still accorded priority, as in the earlier study, but parents could also start to fulfil their own needs, especially when children were older. Children were happier because of material benefits, but there were still tensions, owing to less parental involvement and attention.

Distribution of income within the household

The uncertainty of the route from income to outcome does not apply only to children. Within the household, who benefits from income can depend on who has access to it, who has power over financial decision-making and/or who is responsible for buying different items. The quantitative analysis of expenditure cited above did examine spending on women's and men's clothing, as well as children's. But other than that, the authors did not dwell on the gender implications of their study. The same is largely true of the FACS research.[27] Yet, as noted, in low-income couples (and in the vast majority of lone-parent families) it is women who are largely responsible for managing income day to day, and income is more likely to be spent on children if directed via the 'purse rather than the wallet'.[28]

Despite this, researchers often do not seem to ask whether increases in couples' incomes arrived via the man or the woman or both, and whether this made any difference to outcomes for children. And many reports are presented as being about 'parents', whereas those interviewed are usually mothers.[29] In addition, findings about the influence of the source and recipient of income on how income is regarded and used[30] have not, by and large, been applied to this area of work. Yet differing perceptions of entitlement and of gender roles – as well as what importance couples accord to sharing resources, regardless of ownership or other criteria – can have implications for how money is used.

However, it is in practice increasingly difficult for researchers to explore these issues in relation to recent benefits and tax credits reforms such as those discussed in some of the studies reported here. This is for several reasons. First, these changes have been complex, with different payments and nominated recipients succeeding one another with great rapidity, and some changes not yet complete. Second, the government's efforts to persuade all claimants to open an account for their benefits/tax credits means that it is now harder to trace their destination than when there was an order book with a priority name. Joint accounts are also common – though researchers have often found that it is access and control that are important, rather than the mere existence of a joint account, when examining distribution of income within the household.[31] Third, tax credits are now jointly owned, whichever partner they are nominally paid to (for example, the 'main carer' for child tax credit).

However, some gender issues relevant to children's wellbeing do emerge from the recent reforms. For example, the man is the claimant in most couples on benefit;[32] one study of couples on benefit found that some male partners used the main benefit for household bills (which men are often responsible for dealing with), with child benefit used for items for children (which women usually pay for).[33] Once the introduction of child tax credit has been completed, most women in couples on income support or jobseeker's allowance are likely to see the income they (are intended to) receive as the nominated 'main carer' increase significantly; many have already done so. Given that adult benefit rates have fallen further and further behind earnings, whereas child tax credit is being increased in line with earnings or even more, will this affect the amount of income spent on items for children? Or on the other hand, will it create a disincentive for 'second earners' to enter the labour market, and therefore reduce the amount potentially available for children? And for those families with an earner, what has been the impact, if any, of the switch away from working tax credit being paid through the pay packet (from April 2006)?[34] Does the fact that some payments are labelled for one partner affect how they are seen and/or used, even if they are paid into a joint account? To date, many questions such as these lack answers.

Some broader issues

Being 'careful with money' is also related to gender, as well as household income. Women in low-income families are often said by their partners to be more skilled at day-to-day financial management, which is in part why they tend to be given that dubious privilege.[35] The FACS research did examine the issue of budgeting skills, which is so often raised in relation to the idea of giving low-income families more income. The researchers were clear that the impact of increased income depended on the family's financial skills.[36] The authors of one study noted that the people who struggled financially were typically lone parents, without a partner's support, but they also listed other factors.[37] The authors of another study found that financial skills seemed to be influenced by experience of dealing with money, access to financial services, family type and involvement with work.[38] Those who did badly appeared to be worse at gauging what income they had. The authors called for initiatives to increase financial skills among those on low income. But it is important to note that there is no suggestion that these parents were not prioritising their children's needs; they were just not as good at managing their money to ensure that the benefits of extra income were realised in full.

This chapter is not seeking to argue that all the problems faced by low-income families can be solved by higher incomes. That would be too simplistic, even leaving aside the issue of differential budgeting skills. The longer-term impact of the stresses caused by poverty on parenting, and on child outcomes – quite apart from other disadvantages suffered disproportionately by families on low incomes – is likely to mean that additional, and more complex, forms of support are required.[39] The authors of one analysis conclude that, given the less than exact fit between low income and (their) measures of hardship, other contributing factors must be in operation: living standards are also constrained by family circumstances and changes. The effects of what they call 'markers of disadvantage' – family break-up, loss of employment, large families, belonging to a minority ethnic group or having poor family health – may not respond to greater financial assistance in the short term, or even the longer term. There is a need to investigate what combination of measures would bring about an optimal improvement in living standards.[40] Piachaud also argues that "more money is not of itself enough to enhance the quality of children's lives".[41] Among other points, he notes that "the needs of children – beyond basic food, clothing and heating – are socially defined" (p. 450), and that commercialisation creates new 'needs' transmitted via television and other media; "limiting the pressures that over-extend needs may be essential if child poverty is to be effectively tackled" (p. 450). Like Piachaud, this chapter argues that additional financial support is not sufficient – but it is essential.

Neither is this chapter arguing that women are always better managers of money than men, or that mothers invariably put their children first. Nonetheless, the evidence about the importance of mothers as a conduit for resources to benefit children is strong. And, given the current pattern of gendered responsibilities within two-parent low-income families in particular, it seems more likely that additional income routed via the 'main carer' will directly benefit the children. Such additional financial support could take various forms, including more opportunities for employment (especially for second earners), higher wages and/or increases in benefits/tax credits. However, this should not be used in isolation from efforts by government and others to further shift the gendered division of labour within families with children towards more equitable roles, which will in the longer term result in significant benefits for men and women – and for children.

Notes

[1] R Lister, *Poverty*, Polity Press, Cambridge, 2004; see also Women's Budget Group, *Women's and Children's Poverty: Making the links*, WBG, London, 2005.

[2] P Gregg, J Waldfogel and E Washbrook, 'That's the way the money goes: expenditure patterns as real incomes rise for the poorest families with children', in J Hills and K Stewart (eds) *A More Equal Society? New Labour, poverty, inequality and exclusion*, The Policy Press, Bristol, 2005, pp. 251–75 (especially p. 273). The data come from the Family Expenditure Survey (1996/97 to 2000/01). See also 'Family expenditures post-welfare reform in the UK: are low-income families

starting to catch up?', *Labour Economics* 13:6 (2006), pp. 721–46, by the same authors, which uses data from 1995–98 and 2000–03, and tests the links between the policy reforms and changes in family expenditures more formally, using more complex research methods and extends the period of analysis. The researchers find broadly similar changes in the spending of low-income families eligible for more financial support to those described here.

[3] See, for example, E Kempson, *Life on a Low Income*, Joseph Rowntree Foundation, York, 1996.

[4] S Middleton, K Ashworth and I Braithwaite, *Small Fortunes*, Joseph Rowntree Foundation, York, 1997.

[5] L Adelman, S Middleton and K Ashworth, *Britain's Poorest Children: Severe and persistent poverty and social exclusion*, Save the Children, London, 2003.

[6] T Ridge, *Childhood Poverty and Social Exclusion: From a child's perspective*, The Policy Press, Bristol, 2002.

[7] See, for example, J Pahl, *Money and Marriage*, Macmillan. London, 1989.

[8] See, for example, Kempson, 1996 (note 3 above); Middleton *et al*, 1997 (note 4 above).

[9] WBG, 2005 (see note 1).

[10] J Goode, C Callender and R Lister, *Purse to Wallet? Gender inequalities and income distribution within families on benefit*, Policy Studies Institute, London, 1998.

[11] E Kempson, *Life on a Low Income*, Joseph Rowntree Foundation, York, 1996.

[12] F Bennett, 'We know who they are, but do we really hear what they have to say?', *Parliamentary Brief*, October 2006.

[13] Kempson, 1996, p. 28 (see note 11).

[14] J Waldfogel, *Welfare Reforms and Child Wellbeing in the US and UK*, CASE paper 126, Centre for the Analysis of Social Exclusion, London School of Economics, London, 2007, p. 5.

[15] Gregg, Waldfodel and Washbrook, 2005, pp. 251–75 (see note 2).

[16] Families in which the main source of income was from self-employment were excluded.

[17] Spending on holidays, although increasing disproportionately for low-income families with young children, was from a very low base, and the absolute difference with high-income families increased.

[18] Waldfogel, 2007 (see note 14). This is based on the 2005 book chapter by Gregg, Waldfogel and Washbrook referred to in note 2 above, in addition to US research.

[19] S Vegeris and J Perry, *Families and Children 2001: Living standards and the children*, Department for Work and Pensions (DWP) Research Report no. 190, Corporate Document Services (CDS), Leeds, 2003. (Note that the authors caution that increases in incomes may be overestimated because the survey was moved from summer to autumn between 1999 and

2001. They also point out that some increase in income is to be expected in a panel survey in which participants are getting older between interviews.)

[20] The authors of the FACS study developed their own measure of hardship, which includes living in poor housing conditions, not being able to manage on one's income, and going without essential items. This results in a scale of nine items; lacking three items or more is an indicator of severe hardship.

[21] The changes they draw attention to over the period of their own study include moves into employment, rises in child benefit and increases in the child premiums in income support, housing benefit and working families tax credit.

[22] C Farrell and W O'Connor, *Low Income Families and Household Spending*, DWP Research Report no. 192, CDS, Leeds, 2003.

[23] Quotas were used for family size and levels of hardship and debt, and the selection of the sample was controlled for location, age of respondent and age of the youngest child.

[24] Lister, 2004 (see note 1); see also Ridge, 2002 (see note 6).

[25] The children of those who felt worse off in paid work in fact lost out, not just because what treats there had been, had been focused on them and were now withdrawn, but because some things given free to those on benefit were not available once their parent(s) were in employment.

[26] J Graham, R Tennant, M Huxley and W O'Connor, *The Role of Work in Low Income Families with Children – A longitudinal qualitative study*, DWP Research Report no. 245, CDS, Leeds, 2005.

[27] Though motivations to take up employment were said to include for some people guilt about reliance on their (new) partner.

[28] Some studies demonstrating this have not been confined to low-income families, and so are not cited here (eg, S J Lundberg, R A Pollak and T J Wales, 'Do husbands and wives pool their resources? Evidence from the UK child benefit', *Journal of Human Resources* 32:3, 1997, pp. 463–80, which examines the switch from (family allowances and) child tax allowances to child benefit in the mid- to late-1970s.

[29] A similar point is made in WBG, 2005 (see note 9).

[30] For example, D Snape and D Molloy with M Kumar, in *Relying on the State, Relying on Each Other*, DWP Research Report no. 103, CDS, Leeds, 1999, find that there is less strong individual ownership of benefits compared with earned income, and that benefit income is valued less than earnings.

[31] See, for example, S Sung and F Bennett, 'Dealing with money in low- to moderate-income couples: insights from individual interviews', in K Clarke, T Maltby and P Kennett (eds) *Social Policy Review 19: Analysis and debate in social policy*, The Policy Press (in association with the Social Policy Association), Bristol, 2007, pp. 151–73.

[32] Women massively outnumber men as partners of claimants for most of the major benefits (see F Bennett, *Gender and Benefits*, Working Paper Series no. 30, Equal Opportunities Commission, Manchester, 2005, especially pp. 55–56).

[33] D Snape and D Molloy with M Kumar, *Relying on the State, Relying on Each Other*, DWP Research Report no. 103, CDS, Leeds, 1999. Gendered patterns of spending for the whole population (from the 1996 Family Expenditure Survey) are examined by J Pahl, in 'The gendering of spending within households', *Radical Statistics*, autumn 2000, pp. 38–48.

[34] Some of these issues, and related questions, are being explored in project 5 of the Gender Equality Network, 'Within Household Inequalities and Public Policy', in which the principal investigators, in addition to Fran Bennett, are Sue Himmelweit (Open University) and Holly Sutherland (University of Essex). The Network (see www.genet.ac.uk) is funded by the Economic and Social Research Council (RES-225-25-2001).

[35] J Pahl, *Money and Marriage*, Macmillan, London, 1989.

[36] Farrell and O'Connor, 2003 (see note 22); Graham, Tennant, Huxley and O'Connor, 2005 (see note 26).

[37] Farrell and O'Connor, 2003 (see note 22).

[38] Graham, Tennant, Huxley and O'Connor, 2005 (see note 26).

[39] I Katz, J Corlyon, V La Placa and S Hunter, *The Relationship Between Parenting and Poverty*, Joseph Rowntree Foundation, York, 2007, cited in J Blewett, 'Poverty and parenting', Community Care, 20 September 2007.

[40] Vegeris and Perry, 2003 (see note 19).

[41] D Piachaud, 'Child poverty, opportunities and quality of life', *Political Quarterly*, 72:4 (2001), pp. 446–53 (especially p. 449).

14 What do we mean by 'adequate' benefits?

John Veit-Wilson

> *"When poor people in my constituency in Croydon come to see me about these issues, they are not saying 'Mr Wicks, Minister, Malcolm, our main demand is we set a scientific measure'. Funnily enough they want jobs, they want decent schools for their children, they want to get on in life.* **They're not worried about academic measures, they're worried about poverty and how to get out of it.** *"*
> (Malcolm Wicks MP, then Parliamentary Secretary to the Department for Work and Pensions, interview on BBC Radio 4 *Inside Money* broadcast 3 August 2002; emphasis added.)

What do we mean by adequate benefits? Like Mr Wicks's constituents, most people do not usually think first about measures but about what it takes to get out of poverty. Adequate benefits should do that, and this chapter is about what adequacy means.

The word 'adequate' means sufficient for purpose, just enough but not necessarily more than enough. No one boasts of having an adequate holiday: it does not mean luxury.[1] But what is the purpose for which it is adequate? 'Benefits' is a general label for a variety of forms of income maintenance that people need temporarily or permanently, not only for interruptions of earnings because of retirement, sickness, invalidity or unemployment, but when there are certain recognised expenses that reduce already low incomes unacceptably, such as housing costs or council tax. Child benefit and tax credits play a similar role, as do the variety of tax allowances that are also known as fiscal welfare benefits. What we call benefits are all those forms of support paid for out of our individual contributions or general taxes that help to support us and others when we have low incomes. Whether that support is adequate cannot be answered in the abstract, nor can it be decided by government decree. Since the support given may vary for each of the benefits mentioned, their adequacy can be understood only in its concrete forms by considering four questions: adequate for what; adequate for whom; adequate for how long; and who says what is adequate?[2]

Adequate for what?

If the objective is to overcome poverty, then we have to know what poverty means. There are many definitions, but most of them agree that people are in poverty when they live below a standard that their society recognises as a reasonable minimum, and when they lack the resources to achieve that standard of living and take full part in their societies, to be socially included, recognised and respected as full members.[3] Those resources may also be various, and both tangible and intangible, but in the commercialised, marketised and consumerised society in which we all live, enough money is indisputably the most important single material resource. The centrality of money income is shown by the responses across the EU to the survey question of what people need for the good life. "Europeans answer this question unanimously: sufficient income, family support and health."[4] Of course many other factors matter as well as adequate incomes, but adequate incomes matter *first*.

According to many international and European conventions, declarations and treaties that the UK has signed and is bound by, human beings have economic and social rights to an adequate income and to social security benefits to guarantee that income (even if those rights are still not treated by statute law and the courts in the same way as the human, civil and political rights are).[5] These documents assert the right to live decently, to have one's human dignity respected, to take part in society without shame. These are the fundamental aspects of what a minimally adequate level of living must allow, and the evidence is incontrovertible that having enough money plays a central role. This is not an argument about what causes poverty; it is a statement about what is essential to overcome it. As W C Fields put it, "a rich man is nothing more than a poor man with money" – we find the same demographic characteristics, personality faults, behaviours and relationships right across society, but having an adequate income negates everything that identifies what we call poverty.

Adequate for whom and for how long?

Benefits must be good enough for everybody who may have to depend on them. People's incomes fluctuate, and dynamic research has shown that nearly half of the population has lived in low-income households for a year or more during the previous ten years.[7] The risks to people's employment caused by changes in the economy, and to retirement by the shortcomings of some occupational pension schemes, mean that many other people may also experience low incomes in the future. In view of this widespread experience, it is the general public's views of what is adequate for each one of them when those risks occur to them that must be decisive. That means adequacy for people in work just as much as for those whose main source of income is benefits. Our European culture is based on the assumption that the normal source of income for those of working age and their dependants should be paid employment, and on beliefs in social and economic incentives to work that require benefit levels to be appreciably lower than earnings. In other words, if we want to know about benefit adequacy, we have first to consider the adequacy of incomes for people in work. If no one, even on the lowest benefits, is to have an income insufficient for social inclusion (which is what the EU recommends[7]), then in order to maintain the differentials the higher levels such as minimum wages (combined with other appropriate family and household benefits) must be more than adequate in terms of the same standards.

But while the standards of adequacy for social inclusion should not differentiate between people in or out of employment, the periods of time over which they are dependent on earnings or on benefits may be different. That could allow governments to use income adequacy standards to set various tiers for the income maintenance system, based on the duration of dependence. In some countries it has been argued that long-term minimum wage rates, as well as benefits for those who are not in the labour market (disabled or retired people), should be set higher than short-term benefits (such as for unemployment or sickness), on the grounds that adequate benefits for short periods can omit allowances for the repair or replacement of household goods or for occasional expenditures such as holidays, which must be included in the normal adequacy standard.[8] Thus, benefit adequacy can be judged by how long people have to live on it, not by who it is for or the contributions they have paid for it.

Adequacy – who says?

A benefit is not adequate just because the government says it is, but only if it reflects the whole population's views of adequacy. Critics of public opinion approaches often dismiss them as subjective, perhaps forgetting that the whole of democratic politics is based on nothing more than the aggregation of many individual subjective views into objective social facts.

Public views of adequate incomes can be surveyed objectively in several ways. One is to ask the public directly about the household income levels at which they can just get by or make ends meet.[9] Another, indirect, method is to survey what the population thinks are the goods, services and experiences that nobody should be without, and then discover statistically the income levels at which, on average, people do not suffer an enforced lack of, say, three or more of the socially defined necessities.[10] Such statistical methods can also be used to analyse the average levels of household income at which the population as a whole actually achieves national standards – for example, of consumption of recommended nutrients,[11] or of health or education. Shopping basket costs (budget) methods are traditional among some researchers,[12] but if the contents of the adequate basket are to reflect the views of the public and not just of experts dictating the budget, then they must be based on intensive small-scale discussion groups (sometimes known as focus groups). These groups must validly represent all sectors of the whole population and work with the experts in such matters as nutrition and health, until agreement is reached on what is just adequate for households of varying size and composition, before it is costed.[13]

These social science methods give reliable figures for what households of varying sizes and compositions need for adequate levels of living under normal long-term conditions, whatever the sources of their incomes. But these findings are not necessarily helpful for the entirely distinct political task of setting the minimum wage rates and benefit levels. At present, governments do this on the basis of their judgements about trends in earnings and prices and what they think business and the Treasury can afford. If they want to take account of adequacy, they must find and set governmental minimum income standards[14] that reflect politically credible evidence of the incomes needed for each of the tiers of the income maintenance system to achieve a minimally adequate level of living. But which survey evidence should they include? A parliamentary committee recommended in 2001 that the government establish a commission to review all the different kinds of evidence and 'triangulate' it to arrive at recommendations for use in setting adequate benefit levels.[15]

The tone of benefit administration

Adequacy for purpose is a matter not only of the cash levels of benefits, but of the 'tone' of their administration. Are they administered and made accessible in ways which respect claimants' human dignity and treat them as 'included' members of society? Volumes of evidence over decades, even centuries, show that this has never been the case for people in poverty in the UK. Welfare rights services, which were developed in the 1960s to improve the tone of administration, continue to be essential because of the shortcomings of the benefit system.

'Adequate tone' requires that no one would remain in ignorance of their rights to benefits, it would be easy to apply for them, and receiving them would not be stigmatising. This is what people expect from all other financial services and there is no excuse for government benefits being administered in ways that leave people unaware of their rights, make it difficult for them to claim benefits, where administrative errors are hard to correct, and where many people feel the means-tests imply that claimants are financially incompetent or worse. Government attempts to improve this image are not helped by negative images of benefit recipients in the mass media, or by cuts in Department for Work and Pensions and HM Revenue and Customs administrative staffing and in funding for local authority, Citizens Advice Bureau and other organisations' welfare rights services, and legal aid.

Are adequate benefits feasible?

All political parties have committed themselves to the abolition of child poverty and, whatever else they do, this necessitates increasing the incomes of households containing children by raising minimum wages, child benefits, tax credits and the other parts of the benefit system to adequacy levels. But because the government has made a commitment to implementing human rights, it must ensure adequate incomes for everybody in the UK. Whether the costs are feasible and taxpayers can afford them is a matter of political priorities.

The Treasury collects taxes to cover the costs not only of welfare benefits but of the loss in national income caused by those tax-deductible allowances – known as fiscal welfare benefits. For any given level of government expenditure, every pound of tax allowance that one income recipient can deduct means that other taxpayers must pay a pound to make up for it. The amounts taxpayers currently spend on these fiscal welfare benefits for high-income recipients would more than cover a significant part of the costs of raising the lowest incomes to adequacy levels. For example, the cost of tax allowances on occupational pension contributions for *higher rate* taxpayers was about £10 billion in 2004/05: this better-off section of the population took 60% of all this tax benefit even though they were only one in eight of all taxpayers receiving it. Adrian Sinfield has calculated that in 2006/07, out of £25 billion in fiscal welfare, some £15 billion went to the better-off higher rate taxpayers.[16] At the same time, the costs of achieving the government's target of halving child poverty by 2010 were calculated at around £4 billion in 2006.[17] This suggests that the problems are not economic (the taxpayers' money is clearly there for benefit expenditures as a whole) but electoral.

Discussion of the affordability of adequate benefits often reveals that people implicitly focus on *who* these benefits are for, rather than *what* they are for. If we want to focus on overcoming poverty, then we have to clear up the confusion between the adequacy of benefits to meet that objective and their adequacy to meet other valid aims, such as fair returns on contributions or equity between fiscal contributors and beneficiaries, some of which are not necessarily incompatible. Affordability for different purposes and sections of the population needs to be clarified and discussed openly in the light of ensuring everyone's rights to an income adequate for social inclusion.

Adequate benefits require government commitment, a body of robust and credible evidence, and an administrative system that treats them as important and their recipients with respect. All of these essentials are both feasible and affordable; the challenge is to achieve them.

Notes

[1] Adrian Sinfield, personal communication.

[2] S Dubnoff, 'How much income is enough? Measuring public judgements', *Public Opinion Quarterly*, 49:3 (1984), pp. 285–99, augmented by J Veit-Wilson, *Setting Adequacy Standards:*

how governments define minimum incomes, Policy Press, Bristol, 1998, p 21. The same questions can be asked about all abstract concepts such as need, sufficient or enough, and adapted for concepts such as tolerable or bearable – or even affordable.

[3] For a recent compendium of approaches, see the entries for 'Poverty' in the *Routledge International Encyclopaedia of Social Policy* (2006) or the *Routledge Encyclopaedia of Social Theory* (2005).

[4] Wissenschaftszentrum Berlin für Sozialforschung (Berlin Centre for Social Science Research), press release summarising the findings of a cross-national study of living conditions in 28 old and new EU countries, 17 June 2004.

[5] See for instance J Veit-Wilson, 'Some social policy implications of a right to social security', in J Van Langendonck (ed) *The Right to Social Security*, Intersentia, Antwerp, 2007, pp. 57–83; A P van der Mei, 'The justiciability of social rights in the European Union', in F Coomans (ed), *Justiciability of Economic and Social Rights*, Intersentia, Antwerp, 2006.

[6] Several sources quoted in J Flaherty, J Veit-Wilson and P Dornan, *Poverty: The facts, 5th edition*, Child Poverty Action Group, London, 2004, p. 47; see also L Leisering and S Leibfried, *Time and Poverty in Western Welfare States: United Germany in Perspective*, Cambridge University Press, Cambridge, 1999.

[7] European Commission, *Joint Report on Social Inclusion*, European Commission, Luxembourg, 2002, p. 27.

[8] For a discussion of tiers, see J Veit-Wilson, *Setting Adequacy Standards: How governments define minimum incomes*, Policy Press, Bristol, 1998, pp. 34–38.

[9] K Van den Bosch, *Identifying the Poor: Using subjective and consensual measures*, Ashgate, Aldershot, 2001.

[10] J Mack and S Lansley chose three because they found that some people right across the income distribution said they lacked one or two socially defined necessities, but three or more deprivation indicators correlated highly with lower incomes: *Poor Britain*, Allen and Unwin, London, 1985, pp. 175–76.

[11] P Townsend, 'Measuring poverty', *British Journal of Sociology*, 5:2 (1954), pp. 130–37.

[12] Starting with B S Rowntree, *Poverty: A Study of Town Life*, Macmillan, London, 1901.

[13] S Middleton, 'Agreeing poverty lines: the development of consensual budget standards methodology', in J Bradshaw and R Sainsbury (eds) *Researching Poverty*, Ashgate, Aldershot, 2000; see also http://www.minimumincomestandard.org/

[14] J Veit-Wilson, *Setting Adequacy Standards: How governments define minimum incomes*, Policy Press, Bristol, 1998; see also entry on 'Minimum Income Standards' in Routledge International Encyclopaedia of Social Policy, 2006.

[15] House of Commons Social Security Committee (eds) *Integrated Child Credit*, HC 72, The Stationery Office, London, 2001, paragraphs 24–25, pp. xii–xiii.

[16] These figures are quoted from A Sinfield, *Memorandum submitted to the House of Commons Work and Pensions Committee inquiry: 'The best start in life? – Alleviating deprivation, improving social mobility and eradicating child poverty'*, September 2007. They are derived from HMRC (Revenue and Customs Statistics 2007, table 1.5 after tax deducted from pensions paid), and *Hansard* (written answer to PQ by Chris Huhne MP, 24 October 2005, col 52W).

[17] M Brewer, J Browne, H Sutherland, *Micro-simulating Child Poverty in 2010 and 2020*, Joseph Rowntree Foundation, York, 2006; however, in 2007 M Brewer and J Browne suggested a slightly lower figure: *Estimates of the Costs of Meeting the Government's Child Poverty Target in 2010/11: Update after the Budget 2007*, Evidence to the Treasury Select Committee, April 2007 (on Institute for Fiscal Studies website: http://www.ifs.org.uk/docs/tsc_note.pdf).

15 The material and psychological importance of decent wages

Brendan Barber

Introduction

> *"Work for those who can, security for those who cannot."*

The ten words that encapsulate the anti-poverty strategy have been repeated so often that no one should be in any doubt about where the government stands. Wages are the route out of poverty; the answer to child poverty is to get parents into jobs, the answer to disabled people's poverty is to eliminate the barriers to employment they face, and the answer to ethnic minority poverty is to bring black and minority ethnic employment rates up to white levels. Even pensioner poverty in the long term is to be reduced by getting people to work longer and save more.

Trades unions mostly go along with this. In 1994 the TUC launched a campaign to return full employment to the centre of economic policy at a time when most politicians thought that was an absurdly unrealistic target; so it is a matter of some pride for the TUC that this is now the buckle that holds together all the key economic and social policies.

No one should be surprised to learn that unions believe in the central importance of work. Work gives us our role in our communities and our status in society, and helps define our identity. Over the last half century we have gradually recognised the importance of unpaid work such as volunteering, housework and parenting, and one of the great undecided issues of our time is the boundary between paid and unpaid work and how they are allocated. That is a vitally important task, but this chapter will concentrate on paid work and the significance of decent pay.

This chapter will examine two aspects of pay: inequality across the economy as a whole, and the impact of inequality within a single organisation. Decent pay is an *absolute* value – we need to tackle low pay; and decent pay is a *relative* value – we need to tackle pay inequality.

Pay and poverty

The government's decision that they would tackle poverty by moving people into paid work was taken such a long time ago that policy papers these days often do not explain why this approach was chosen. There were two main reasons:[1]

- There was a strong link between worklessness and low incomes (with an even stronger link for *persistent* low incomes).
- The most common routes out of low income were to get a job or to increase earnings.

It is still true that children living in households where none of the adults has a job face a much higher risk of poverty than other children. Data show that 78% of children in families where none of the adults has a job are poor; this compares with 37% of children in families where some but not all of the adults have jobs and just 12% of children in families where all the adults have jobs.[2]

So there is a strong justification for focusing on worklessness, but in-work poverty is at least as important. Most families have at least one adult in employment, and workless families are actually quite a small minority. This means that, despite their much lower *risk* of poverty, families with people in jobs account for a higher *absolute* number of children in poverty: 2.1 million, compared with 1.6 million in workless families.[3] And we know that, although it is true that children in workless families often escape poverty when one of their parents gets a job, there is a large minority who don't escape poverty – about one in three.[4]

Low pay makes parenting much more difficult, because low-paid workers have to work extra-long hours to earn enough to provide for their children. A study of low-paid workers in east London found that they had to work for 60 hours a week to earn about £250, with several of the workers in the study taking on a second job to make ends meet.[5]

In other words, low pay isn't just a problem for the workers with low earnings; it is a major obstacle to the government's plans for ending child poverty. And there are other dimensions of inequality and exclusion where success will depend on the elimination of low pay.

Pay and inequality

First, it is impossible to talk about low pay and in-work poverty without recognising the racial dimension of the problem. Lisa Harker, when researching for the Department for Work and Pensions (DWP) what it would take to end child poverty, noted that "nearly half of children in Pakistani and Bangladeshi families reliant on a single full-time earner are in poverty compared to just 12 per cent of children in white families. The particularly low levels of pay found among Bangladeshi men are likely to explain this heightened risk."[6] A study of low pay in London found that low-paid work was overwhelmingly dominated by migrant workers, half of whom had arrived in the UK in the previous five years. Just over half came from Africa, and only 8.5% described themselves as white British.[7]

There is also a link between low pay, gender and part-time work, as revealed by the figures for workers earning the national minimum wage (NMW):[8]

Share of NMW workers	
Women full-time	19%
Women part-time	47%
Men part-time	13%
Men full-time	21%

Low pay is at the heart of racial and gender inequality, and low-paid workers are also likely to face other problems as well. Three-fifths of low-paid workers in the London study did not receive maternity or paternity leave, half had no annual pay rise (one-third had *never* had a pay rise), most did not receive a premium rate for overtime work, half went unpaid if they had to take time off for an emergency and just over half received no sick pay. Two-thirds received only the minimum statutory entitlement to holidays (or less) and 70% had no occupational pension.[9]

Pay and status

Low-paid jobs are notorious for their low status and the lack of respect workers receive. The east London study noted that "workers complained of a lack of respect from managers".[10] There has always been a tendency to judge people's worth as individuals on the basis of how much they are paid, and the association of low pay with migrant workers, ethnic minorities and women increases this process of downgrading the people who do low-paid work.

And this leads us straight into the second aspect of pay: the matter of comparisons. Decent wages are important because we can be hurt by poverty, but we can just as easily be hurt by *inequality*.

In a certain sense this is not news. Obviously, people who suffer in-work poverty face the diseases and other drawbacks of poverty to a greater extent than higher-paid workers. And it is almost as much of a truism to point out that they have the least freedom to choose alternative jobs, and the most difficulty in escaping dangerous work. It has always been true that low-paid workers are the most likely to have jobs that are demeaning, dangerous and unhealthy.

This is an important issue for unions, and raising health and safety standards continues to be one of their most important achievements. But it is important to understand also how the inequality itself harms people.

Michael Marmot, Britain's leading epidemiologist, has described the links between low status and poor health. In his famous Whitehall studies of civil servants (1967–85) he showed that, contrary to preconceptions about stressed-out senior managers, clerks and messengers were actually far more likely than the 'mandarinate' to suffer the diseases associated with stress. His studies revealed a clear 'social gradient' in life expectancy among civil servants: the higher your grade, the longer you are likely to live.

Marmot has shown how "sustained, chronic and long-term stress is linked to low control over life circumstances", which in turn is linked to low social status, and not just for civil servants: the 'social gradient' can be found in many industries and occupations.[11] The Whitehall study continues to reveal links between inequality at work and poor health. One recent report based on this data revealed a link between unfairness and heart disease, including fatal coronary heart disease, with people who agreed with the statement "I often have the feeling that I am being treated unfairly" being more likely to suffer these outcomes.[12]

Pay and dignity

Decent work is not just a matter of decent pay; it is about dignity at work, and unfairness is a common complaint of people whose jobs are low paid and low in status. A concern with 'fairness' seems to be as strongly embedded in human nature as sensitivity to status. Empirical research has shown that people will sacrifice income to make sure that a smaller total income is divided fairly.[13] It should not surprise us that being the victim of unfair treatment is as stressful as low status.

There is a certain common ground that covers our concerns about low pay, low status and unfairness. In principle low-paid jobs can be of high status and high-paid jobs can be of low status, but this is the exception rather than the rule.

Even when an employer believes that their low-paid members of staff are well respected, workers with comparatively low pay are still likely to see themselves as having low status. This chapter has already noted how our jobs help define us: they characterise our contribution to society, establish our place in both geographical and occupational networks and help us to define ourselves to ourselves. One of the characteristic features of modern societies is the importance of wages in all of this. For all the lip-service that is given to unpaid voluntary and caring work, it is paid work that the government values in its welfare-to-work strategy and young people are encouraged to judge jobs by the pay they attract, rather than the broader contribution they make. Polly Toynbee has pointed out that wages are often taken as a measure of a person's worth in meritocratic societies like ours.[14] Not so long ago, one was much less likely to hear of people being measured by their wages, and this was often referred to as an 'American habit'. Not any more; now it's a normal British approach.

In these circumstances it would be amazing if people did not judge their status by reference to their pay level. There is certainly evidence to support this belief. In the 1990s Andrew Oswald and Andrew Clark used data from the British Household Panel study to look at workers' levels of satisfaction with their jobs, and found that these were more closely linked to their comparative rates than to their absolute levels – someone whose pay level was comparatively low in their particular workplace was more likely to be dissatisfied than someone with earnings that were low when seen in the context of the overall income distribution.

More recently a larger study found that satisfaction depends "not simply upon relative pay but on an individual's *ordinal rank* within a comparison group (for example, whether the individual is 4th or 34th in the wage hierarchy of the company)."[15]

Unions and decent pay

Clearly, decent pay is important from an anti-poverty perspective and as one of the elements of a society that treats everyone with respect. And it is here that unions can have a significant impact. In their day-to-day work, bargaining on behalf of workers, they protect workers from negative fluctuations in their wages during economically tough times;[16] and it is clear that pay is more equal in firms where unions are strong and collective bargaining covers more workers.[17]

Unions can also play a role in policy debates. Through its campaign for the national minimum wage, the TUC has already helped more than a million workers, who get a pay increase each time the rate is raised.[18] The TUC is particularly concerned about the position of vulnerable workers, who rarely receive decent wages and are in the most insecure jobs, receiving the worst treatment. In 2007 it established a Commission on Vulnerable Employment to report (in 2008) on the ways in which government, civil society organisations, employers and trade unions can all improve the lives of vulnerable workers. One of the early lessons learned by the Commission is that some groups, such as some migrant and agency workers, are particularly likely to be denied their rights to statutory minimum standards such as the minimum wage and protection against discrimination. The connection between low pay, low status and exploitation is more than a theory, it is a reality across this country. Any concerted effort to tackle poverty and social exclusion will have to add in-work poverty to the list of evils that must be tackled.

Notes

[1] The Treasury's 1999 report, *Tackling Poverty and Extending Opportunity* remains the best source. See Chapter 2, available at http://www.hm-treasury.gov.uk/media/D/6/734F8D63-BCDC-D4B3-1A9CD199A7DF8D3E.pdf

[2] Department for Work and Pensions (DWP), *Households Below Average Income 1994/5 – 2005/6*, DWP, 2007, table 4.5, available at http://www.dwp.gov.uk/asd/hbai/hbai2006/chapters.asp

[3] Calculated from Table 4.3 in DWP, 2007 (see note 2).

[4] L Harker, *Delivering on Child Poverty: What would it take?*, DWP, 2006, p. 38.

[5] J Wills, *Mapping Low Pay in East London*, QMUL for UNISON and TELCO, 2001, p. 3.

[6] Wills, 2001, p. 29 (see note 5).

[7] Y Evans *et al*, *Making the City Work: Low paid employment in London*, QMUL, 2005, pp. 10–11.

[8] Low Pay Commission, *National Minimum Wage*, 2007, fig. 2.8. Available at http://www.lowpay.gov.uk/lowpay/report/pdf/6828-DTi-Low_Pay_Complete.pdf

[9] Evans *et al*, 2007, p. 13 (see note 7).

[10] Wills, 2001, p. 3 (see note 5).

[11] M Marmot, *Status Syndrome*, Bloomsbury, London, 2004.

[12] R de Vogli, J E Ferrie, T Chandola, M Kivimaki and M Marmot, 'Unfairness and health: evidence from the Whitehall II study', *J. Epidemiol. Community Health*, 61 (2007), pp. 513–18.

[13] The classic experiment demonstrating this is the 'ultimatum game': there are two players, one is given a sum of money which they have to share with the other player in any proportions they choose; the other can accept this division, or reject it – in which case neither player gets anything. Economic theory predicts that the second player should accept any positive offer as being better than the alternative. In fact, most people reject offers of less than one-third. R H Frank, T Gilovich and D T Regan, 'Does Studying Economics Inhibit Cooperation?", Journal of Economic Perspectives, 7:2 (1993), pp. 159–171.

[14] Polly Toynbee, *Hard Work: Life in low pay Britain*, Bloomsbury, London, 2003.

[15] G D A Brown, J Gardner, A Oswald and Jing Qian, *Does Wage Rank Affect Employees' Wellbeing?*, IZA Discussion Paper no. 1505, Institute for the Study of Labour, Bonn, 2005.

[16] A Bryson and J Forth, *The Theory and Practice of Pay Setting*, NIESR Dicussion Paper no. 285, 2006, available at http://www.niesr.ac.uk/pubs/dps/DP285.pdf

[17] D Metcalf, K Hansen and A Charlwood, 'Unions And The Sword Of Justice: Unions And Pay Systems, Pay Inequality, Pay Discrimination And Low Pay', *National Institute Economic Review*, No. 176, April 2001, pp. 61–75. Unions reduce the male–female wage differential by 2.6%, the black–white differential by 1.4% and the manual–non-manual differential by 3.1%.

[18] Low Pay Commission, *National Minimum Wage*, 2007. Available at http://www.lowpay.gov.uk/lowpay/report/pdf/6828-DTi-Low_Pay_Complete.pdf

Conclusion

Towards eradicating child poverty

Jason Strelitz and Ruth Lister

What drives the experience of poverty in the UK? The evidence and arguments presented in this book highlight how so much of the experience of poverty is about lack of income. Low income pervades much of parents' and children's lives, imposing constraints and penalties, which can have a deeply harmful impact on children's wellbeing and life chances.

It is worth reminding ourselves about some of the realities of child poverty in the UK:

- The majority of children in poverty are in a household where someone is in work. Given that many on low incomes are subject to the 'low pay, no pay' cycle, moving in and out of low-paid work, the proportion of children in poverty with parents totally disconnected from the labour market is low.
- The majority of children living in poverty are in two-parent households: 58% in total. As with people's employment lives, domestic lives change; few children in poverty spend the majority of their childhood years in lone-parent households. Nevertheless, children in lone-parent families are particularly vulnerable to poverty.
- Some 85% of children in poverty are in a household with between one and three children. Although being in a large family is a risk factor for poverty, children living in large families are in the minority.
- About 30% of children in poverty are in a household where at least one adult or child has a disability, making the risk of poverty significantly higher.
- The vast majority of children in poverty in the UK are defined as 'white British'. However, even though children from minority ethnic groups are very much a minority, they face a significantly higher risk of poverty.

Popular images of what poverty looks like in the UK are different from the reality on the ground. The experience of poverty is one of vulnerability: lacking security and support, people desperately try to gather and deploy the resources necessary to provide for their family's needs in a world that is often uncompromising and hostile.

At the centre of that experience of poverty is lack of income. The benefits and tax credits that millions of people rely on take no account of people's actual need. As Jonathan Bradshaw writes in Chapter 12, "There is no rationale for the differentials in the level of benefits. There is no basis in need, justice or equity; no basis in concerns about incentives." The result is that low-income families face tough choices about how to make ends meet from one week to the next. For example, as Liz Dowler points out in Chapter 4, "Poorer households spend a much higher proportion of income on food than the richest households (about twice as high), although the actual amount they spend is considerably lower... Food is usually where people have to cut back to meet these pressing demands on their purse."

The struggle to get by in poverty is graphically illustrated in Chapter 1, where parents speak about how they juggle resources and the sacrifices involved. Too often this struggle to make ends meet results in debt. As Stephen Mckay and Karen Rowlingson write in Chapter 6, "... 42% of those in poverty were seriously behind with repaying bills or credit commitments in the previous year (compared with 4% among the non-poor". The impact of debt can be severe, inflicting greater financial penalties on the poorest households, firstly through interest payments and penalty charges, and potentially through the courts; ultimately, arrears can result in disconnections and repossessions. The impact of debt is exacerbated by a poverty premium. Claire Kober explains in Chapter 7 how "low-income consumers pay a premium of about £1,000 a year in acquiring cash and credit, and in purchasing goods and services". The poorest households often pay more for gas, electricity and insurance and to obtain credit – for example, home credit companies such as Provident offer loans at over 180% annual percentage rate (APR).

The cumulative impact of poverty on people's psychological wellbeing is immense. Avril Mewse and colleagues write in Chapter 9: "Despite people's efforts to buffer the impacts of poverty, economic hardship has an adverse effect on psychological wellbeing. Poverty is both a cause and a consequence of poor mental health." But the impact goes wider still. Matt Davies explains in Chapter 10 that "one of the most drastic consequences is the sense of isolation and exclusion associated with poverty, exacerbated by a sense of stigma and shame". Low pay, too, can represent an assault on the dignity of workers, as argued by Brendan Barber in Chapter 15.

Other chapters in the book highlight a number of further consequences of poverty in the UK. Tania Burchardt and Asghar Zaidi show in Chapter 3 the immense hidden poverty in families where there are children with disabilities. The extra costs that these families face are not accounted for in national poverty figures, yet their cost of living is much higher. A lone parent with a child with a disability on average needs to have an income 20% higher than a family without, to have the same standard of living. Paul Gregg reveals the dramatic impact that rises in family incomes can have on children's outcomes. Statistical analysis shows a direct effect with improvements in educational outcomes; half of the educational inequality in the UK, the gap in attainment between rich and poor, stems from differences in income.

While we typically think of poverty in terms of the material constraints it imposes on people, David Piachaud highlights the impact on people's time, 'the ultimate scarce resource'. Those on low wages must often work long and antisocial hours to make ends meet and are less likely to have access to the time-saving devices or services which the more affluent use. Lesley Hoggart and Sandra Vegeris demonstrate the difficulties many lone parents face in going into work. They show how many lone parents find it very difficult to balance the conflict between the low pay associated with part-time work and the inability to provide sufficient care for their children if working full-time.

There is much talk from policy-makers about the need to foster aspirations among those living in poverty in the UK. But such talk often fails to recognise the extent to which people in poverty do have aspirations, especially for their children on the one hand and the immense constraints on their lives on the other. As Gabrielle Preston argues in Chapter 2, the education system all too often places barriers in the way of children in poverty, rather than offering them ladders out. The package of low-paid and unstable work, together with means-tested support available to those with few skills and qualifications, alongside high childcare and housing costs, means that work is unsustainable for many people living on benefits who have significant caring responsibilities or disabilities themselves. Increasing people's aspirations is not about persuading them 'to want a better life', but about helping them to tackle the real barriers they face in many aspects of their lives.

Where next for policy?

Article 27 of the United Nations Convention on the Rights of the Child 1989 says that:

> *"States Parties recognize the right of every child to a standard of living adequate for the child's physical, mental, spiritual, moral and social development."*

The evidence set out in this book suggests that the impact of increased incomes on children's standard of living and, hence, their development could be immediate. More money for necessities, adequate nutritious food, decent clothes and shoes, more activities and lower stress levels in the family home could all contribute to immediate life improvements for children and their parents. As Fran Bennett shows in Chapter 13, as families have seen their incomes rise in recent years, they have spent more on those necessities. Beyond this, however, the evidence would suggest significant long-term effects. If it is persistent poverty which has the harshest impact on children's lives, the corollary is that persistent decent incomes result in far superior outcomes for children. The hugely unequal outcomes for poor children, evident in the government's Opportunity for All statistics or the Joseph Rowntree Foundation's Monitoring Poverty and Social Exclusion reports across all aspects of children's lives, have resulted from many years of millions of children living in poverty, with resources far below the levels enjoyed by the mainstream. The cumulative impact for children has been substantial. The 2007 Unicef report on child wellbeing in developed countries shows the UK at the bottom, directly as a result of decades of high levels of child poverty. Those countries at the top of the tables across many areas of children's wellbeing are those that have supported family incomes to an adequate level.

Addressing this issue in a sustained way over the next decade in order to eradicate child poverty in the UK will, in turn, lead to systematic improvement in the standard of living and life chances for millions of children in the UK. There is no silver bullet for tackling child poverty; the multiple consequences of decades of inequality have created a complex issue. Early years interventions, a focus on the attainment gap, financial inclusion policy, and programmes helping people back into work are among a plethora of important areas. The role of this book is not to go over the ground that has been much documented elsewhere, not least in the government's various strategy documents on child poverty.

However, the evidence in this book does point to one intervention that could have the biggest impact: improving incomes. The government recognises the importance of this: their Public Service Agreement to "halve the number of children in poverty by 2010-11, on the way to eradicating child poverty by 2020" states that:

> *"Reducing poverty through raising incomes: reform of the provision of financial support for families has been a key driver behind the fall to date in the number of children in relative low-income households. The Government's support will continue to be based on the principle of progressive universalism – help for all, and extra help for those who need it most."*

However, at present there is no promise of any significant improvements in the level of this support.

Invest £4 billion where it matters

Research by the Joseph Rowntree Foundation, based on modelling by the Institute for Fiscal Studies, showed that the government would need to spend £4.5 billion extra per year – closely aimed at particular tax credits – to meet the target of halving child poverty by 2010. After the 2007 Budget, which directed some extra resources into child benefit and tax credits, the estimate now is that £4 billion a year will be needed. The Campaign to End Child Poverty is calling for these resources to be invested in child benefit and child tax credits as a matter of urgency. These resources will begin to narrow the gap between the incomes of those who rely on benefit and tax credits and the poverty line. They must be directed at all children living in poverty, ensuring that those with the lowest incomes, typically those relying on out-of-work benefits, see their incomes rise.

In addition, the poverty of children cannot be divorced from that of their parents. It is also essential, therefore, that the adult rates of out-of-work benefits are increased in real terms, as further improvements in financial support for children cannot on their own lift significant numbers of families on benefit out of poverty.

As John Veit-Wilson argues in Chapter 14:

> *"... according to many international and European conventions, declarations and treaties that the UK has signed and is bound by, human beings have*

economic and social rights to an adequate income and to social security benefits to guarantee it… These documents assert the right to live decently, to have one's human dignity respected, to take part in society without shame. These are the fundamental aspects of what a minimally adequate level of living must allow, and the evidence is incontrovertible that having enough money plays a central role."

Both he and Jonathan Bradshaw (in Chapter 12) make the case for minimum income standards as a benchmark of adequacy and decency.

Save the Children, along with a wide range of other organisations, believes that the government should introduce seasonal grants for low-income families. These would be lump sum payments, which would help families with expensive items and the particular costs associated with winter and summer time. Research with low-income families has shown that 70% would prefer two lump sums over equivalent small rises in their weekly incomes.[1] Access to lump sums would give low-income families some choices about how to deploy their resources, something they often lack, given the constant struggle to make ends meet.[2]

Improving pay and security for the low paid

A great challenge for our society is how to enhance the security, pay and conditions of those in low-skilled work. For most people work must remain the most sustainable route out of poverty, but, as noted above, just over half of children in poverty are in a household where someone works. While reform will be piecemeal by its nature, it must be underpinned by a vision of what work should mean for all citizens, including those with the fewest employment opportunities.

Important initiatives, such as the TUC's Commission on Vulnerable Employment, will undoubtedly make valuable recommendations as to how to achieve these goals, aside from ensuring that the value of the minimum wage is increased and maintained relative to average wages. Dreams of a universal, high-skilled new economy notwithstanding, low-skilled, part-time, temporary work is not going to disappear over the next decade. Indeed, many millions of people will continue to rely on it, so critical areas must include:
- extending the rights of agency and migrant workers

- effective enforcement of employment law to ensure that rights in respect of the minimum wage and other working conditions are met
- an improvement in the status of part-time work
- extending the right to request flexible working
- being fully committed to the adults' skills agenda, emerging from the Leitch review, so as to create a real offer of training that matches the needs and aspirations of adults with low skills.

Tackling the poverty premium

Maximising the resources that families have does not only mean ensuring that their incomes are sufficient; it means tackling some of the penalties they face in their outgoings. A Poverty Premium Index, whereby the government monitored the extra penalties faced by poor households, would be a start to addressing them. Critical elements of tacking the poverty premium include:

- reform of the social fund, to create a much more widely available source of affordable credit for low-income households. This could be developed with the assistance of the banks and credit union movement
- action by providers of basic services, critically gas and electricity companies, must close the gap between the cost of different payment methods to ensure that all families have access to the cheapest tariffs and costs.

Ensuring that the extra costs of disability are recognised

Measuring poverty solely in terms of an indicator that recognises household size and children's age but takes no account of the extra costs associated with disability will inevitably hide real poverty. The government should adapt its measure of poverty when applied to households containing a child or adult with disabilities in order to reflect these additional costs.

Commitments for 2020

Each budget and pre-budget statement sees anti-poverty charities, trade unions and other organisations calling on the government to invest more in supporting incomes of the poorest. There is of course more for the government to do to close the gap between the incomes of the poorest and average incomes, but such twice-yearly bouts are not a sustainable solution to ensuring a society free from poverty. Over the period to 2020, by which time the government hopes to have abolished child poverty, at a minimum the incomes of the poorest must rise with average incomes. Otherwise rates of poverty will rise again. This means that the incomes that people rely on – out-of-work benefits, child-related benefits, disability-related support, tax credits and the minimum wage – must rise at least in line with average earnings. As stated above, this should include adult-related benefits, which have seen their relative value plummet over the past decade. A commitment to such a sustainable strategy is critical to ensuring that the government achieves its goal to eradicate child poverty by 2020.

Money matters. That is why our primary measures of poverty are based on household income. The evidence in this book shows clearly how inadequate material resources adversely affect parents and children in their homes, neighbourhoods, schools and workplaces. Poverty has implications for education, housing, neighbourhood environment and health, and it may have an impact on people's sense of self-worth and efficacy and their life strategies. But these impacts cannot be separated from the central issue of income. Increasing the incomes of the poorest families, persistently and securely, will have the most significant impact on the quality of life and the life chances of millions of children in the UK. We urge the government to go further and faster in meeting its commitments to these children.

Notes

[1] YouGov survey of low-income families for Save the Children, April 2007

[2] T Smeeding, K R Phillips and M O'Connor, 'The EITC: Expectation, knowledge, use and economic and social mobility', *National Tax Journal*, 53: 1187–1209, US General Accounting Office, 2000

The Well-being of Children in the UK
Second edition

Edited by Jonathan Bradshaw and Emese Mayhew

"an invaluable resource"
Journal of Child Health Care

"an essential research tool for academics, policy-makers and campaigners"
ChildRight magazine

The *Well-being of Children in the UK* (second edition) offers a unique collection of evidence on the physical, cognitive, behavioural and emotional well-being of children in the UK. It covers all aspects of well-being identified in the government's Children and Young People's Framework:
- economic well-being: children poverty and children's environments
- being healthy: physical and mental health, and children's lifestyles
- staying safe: maltreatment, substitute care and crime
- enjoying and achieving: children's time and space, childcare and educational achievement
- making a positive contribution.

2005; ISBN 1 84187 101 X

£19.95

See overleaf on how to order.

To order more copies of *Why Money Matters* or any other Save the Children publications:

- visit www.savethechildren.org.uk
- telephone NBN International on 01752 202301
- email: orders@nbninternational.com

For more information or a copy of Save the Children's publications catalogue, phone 020 7012 6400.